FAMOUS AIRCRAFT OF THE
NATIONAL AIR AND SPACE MUSEUM

Bellanca C. F.

The Emergence of the Cabin Monoplane in the United States

by Jay P. Spenser

PUBLISHED FOR THE

National Air and Space Museum

BY THE

Smithsonian Institution Press

WASHINGTON, D.C.

1982

Cover art by John F. Amendola, Jr.

FRONTISPIECE:
The recently completed Bellanca C.F. basks in the sun in the summer of 1922. (Ernest Bihler via John Underwood)

Unless otherwise indicated, all photographs are from the files of the National Air and Space Museum.

Library of Congress Cataloging in Publication Data

Spenser, Jay P.
    Bellanca C.F.: the emergence of the cabin monoplane in the United States.

    (Famous aircraft of the National Air and Space Museum; v. 6)
    1. Bellanca airplanes. I. National Air and Space Museum. II. Title. III. Title: Bellanca CF. IV. Series,
TL686.B4S63   629.133'343   81-607557
    ISBN 0-87474-881-X   AACR2

The paper in this book meets the guidelines for permanence and durability of the Committee on Production Guidelines for Book Longevity of the Council on Library Resources.

Contents

Foreword

Jay Spenser's account of the Bellanca C.F., a remarkable but virtually unknown airplane, fills a gap in aviation history.

Little has been written about Giuseppe Bellanca, yet he made major contributions to both aviation technology and aviation history. His sturdy high-wing monoplanes, starting with the Bellanca C.F., set records for endurance and efficiency and were used on many of the important long-range flights in the 1920s and 1930s. Clarence Chamberlin's 1927 nonstop flight from New York to Berlin and the Pangborn-Herndon 1931 nonstop flight from Japan to the United States are but two examples of the dependability of Bellanca's designs.

In this carefully researched volume, Jay Spenser relates not only the history of the C.F., first in the famous line, but the history of Bellanca's company and his other aircraft, as well as the careers of some of the pilots. Most of the photographs in the book have never before been published. Also included are the details of the restoration of the C.F. by Garber Facility technicians, and drawings and photographs that will be of particular interest to the model builder.

DONALD S. LOPEZ
Chairman, Aeronautics Department
National Air and Space Museum

Acknowledgments

Heartfelt thanks are due to a variety of individuals in the preparation of this book. First and foremost, the author wishes to express his gratitude to August T. Bellanca and his family for their gracious hospitality and trust. Access was granted to all the papers of G. M. Bellanca, materials were kindly lent, and questions were answered at every turn.

Without the boundless help of John W. Underwood, eminent aviation historian and writer, this book would have been far less satisfactory; a wealth of rare photographs was provided, as well as the results of many years of tireless research, and constructive advice. Equally deserving of thanks is Peter M. Bowers, an historian without peer and walking encyclopedia who also turned his editor's eye to the thankless task of helping the author appear literate.

Additionally, thanks are due to Walter J. Addems, Dana Bell, Louis R. Berlepsch, Warren Bodie, Walter J. Boyne, Kathleen Brooks-Pazmany, Susan Brown, George H. Clapp, Dorothy S. Cochrane, Tom D. Crouch, the Federal Aviation Administration Aircraft Registration Branch, Von D. Hardesty, Karl Heinzel, Richard D. Horigan, Jr., ace photographer Dale Hrabak, William K. Kaiser of the Cradle of Aviation Museum, Paul Kotze, Donald S. Lopez, Robert B. Meyer, Robert C. Mikesh, Claudia M. Oakes, Theron Rinehart and the Fairchild Republic Company, Bill Stevenson, Gordon Swanborough, and U.S. Air Force Photo. To Susan L. Owen, who typed the manuscript with accuracy and aplomb, and to editor John Harris of the Smithsonian Institution Press, the author expresses boundless gratitude.

Bellanca C.F.

Introduction

The Bellanca C.F. landed and rolled to a stop in a field near Omaha, Nebraska. There was only a small crowd present to witness the conclusion of the first flight of an airplane that would quietly change the face of aviation in the United States. It was an elegant monoplane with a high wing, lifting struts, and a fully enclosed passenger cabin. Ironically, the flight went largely unheralded by both the press and the public; only Giuseppe Mario Bellanca himself had an inkling of the significance of his creation.

It was June 8, 1922, a time when American flying fields were dominated by biplanes of limited performance, such as the Curtiss JN-4 and Standard J-1. World War I had been over less than four years and aviation was taking its first faltering steps toward practical airline service. Against this backdrop, the first flight of the C.F. represented a major advance. America was a land where performance was the greatest single measure of worth, and this pioneering aircraft was to enjoy wide recognition early in its career.

Fame was short-lived for the Bellanca C.F., however. After a spectacular, unbroken series of first-place wins at a variety of air meets, the aircraft was quickly forgotten. Ironically, as the name of its designer became ever better known, the C.F. lapsed into even deeper obscurity. The later *Columbia* is the Bellanca that is today generally remembered, although it first flew four years after the C.F. This earlier aircraft went on to lead a picaresque existence through a variety of owners, was substantially modified, and had already been in one air museum before eventually coming to rest in the National Air and Space Museum in Washington, D.C.

A distinction must be drawn between capricious fame and historical significance, and there are two reasons why the long-overlooked Bellanca C.F. has been selected for inclusion in the National Aeronautical Collection of the Smithsonian Institution. First, it was unquestionably the most efficient airplane in existence at the time of its first flight, with such excellent performance that even by today's standards it is little short of astounding. The basis for such a sweeping statement will be presented later in this book.

Second, it was the earliest in the first successful line of cabin monoplanes in the United States. The combination of an enclosed passenger cabin and a single wing has since been all but universally adopted in commercial, military, and general aviation. The only concession to the World War I generation of pilots, who claimed they could not fly aithout the wind at their cheek, was the placement of the pilot in an open cockpit aft of the passenger cabin instead of at the front as one might logically expect.

The history of this unique aircraft, the revolution in design and performance that it helped bring about, and its globe-trotting descendants, will be described in the first five chapters of this book. A look at its later life and restoration by museum craftsmen will follow in the two concluding chapters. It is hoped that this study of the earliest Bellanca cabin monoplane will help this aircraft to regain the recognition it so richly deserves.

While in his midtwenties, Bellanca constructed a parasol-wing monoplane in which he taught himself to fly. He then opened a flying school on Long Island, which operated from 1912 through 1915. Among his students was New York's famous mayor, Fiorello H. LaGuardia. (Courtesy August T. Bellanca)

Origins of the Bellanca C.F.

The temptation is strong to think of an airplane as something more than just an arrangement of wood, metal, and fabric. Machines that fly capture the imagination as few other inanimate objects can, allowing the human spirit to soar in the age-old dream of flight. Rare is the pilot who can remain unaffected by the shared intimacy of sky, cloud, and sunlight above the earth, or free of an affectionate bond for the instrument that makes it possible. Even the most analytic mind will succumb to the poetic allure of these elements and begin to impute distinctive personality traits to the machine. Airplanes, especially the older ones, demand a deference usually accorded to living beings.

The danger in such anthropomorphizing is that one tends to accept an airplane *prima facie* instead of viewing it as an expression of a designer's skill and personality. From preliminary sketches to flying machine is an arduous process, one in which myriad choices are at hand and each decision affects all the others. True engineering skill was rare in the early decades of aviation; true genius was rarer still. Among the latter group, one might name Junkers and Rohrbach in Germany, de Havilland and Short in England, and Vought and Douglas in the United States. One would also have to name Bellanca.

Giuseppe Mario Bellanca was born on March 19, 1886, the son of a miller in the Sicilian village of Sciacca. Called "Pepino" by his family, he grew up fascinated by the natural world around him. He lived on hilly slopes overlooking the Mediterranean, where the constant breezes from the sea caught and held his attention. There were the seagulls that swung and soared so deftly, there were the kites the boy constructed and flew, and there were the discarded fragments from a local pottery that he tossed by the hour from the cliffs. All revealed the atmosphere to be a dynamic and fluid medium.

"I can see air," he once proclaimed.

Bellanca traveled to Milan to attend the Technical Institute, where he obtained a teaching certificate in mathematics, a subject for which he had a special affinity. An early determination to be an efficiency consultant to businesses gave way to his greater interest, however, and he continued his studies at the *Politecnico* from which he graduated in 1910 with a degree in engineering and mathematics.

It was during his studies that his love of flight came to the fore. He did not at once hear of the accomplishments of the Wright brothers in America, much of whose activity was conducted in secret while patent applications were pending, nor of their vehicle. More immediately observable were the efforts of Europeans, especially the French. News of the Wrights, Glenn Curtiss, and a spectacular flight in the summer of 1908 by Delagrange excited the twenty-two-year-old student, and he decided to dedicate himself to similar experimentation.

Such work was beyond the means of a student, so Bellanca took on two partners. He wanted to design a tractor airplane, but he was outvoted, and the machine ended up being a pusher much like the Wright Flyer. Of the three partners, Enea Bossi won the privilege of acting as test pilot, and the plane's

20-hp Zust engine lifted him off Baggio Field on December 8, 1909. A new design flown by an enthusiastic but totally inexperienced pilot is a poor combination, and the result was as might be expected. Bossi was not hurt in the ensuing crash, but the plane was destroyed.

Although of short duration, this was the first flight of a totally Italian-designed and -built airplane. Bossi, who was awarded a medal and pilot's certificate number 2 by his country, went on to design seaplanes for the military before immigrating to the United States in 1918, where he worked in the aviation industry.

While Giuseppe Bellanca gained less experience than he had hoped with this project, it nevertheless served to strengthen his resolve to make aviation his career. He and the third member of the original partnership, Paolo Invernizzi, decided to construct a plane Ballanca had originally conceived a year before in response to the *London Daily Mail*'s much-discussed offer of £1,000 for the first pilot of any nationality to fly across the English Channel. Louis Blériot accomplished this feat, winning the prize and international acclaim early on the morning of July 15, 1909, in his delicate Blériot XI monoplane.[1]

Although the monetary incentive was gone, the tractor biplane was still built. Interesting in that it featured a profusion of horizontal and vertical tail surfaces, this plane was unfortunately never tested, as the partners lacked money for an engine. The eventual fate of this tractor is not known.

Fortunately, Bellanca had the support of his family in the profession to which he chose to devote himself. In 1911, he came to America with his parents, five brothers, and sister, settling in Brooklyn, New York. It was a heady environment for young Bellanca, for the Long Island flying fields were within easy reach. Not content merely to watch the pioneer aviators, Giuseppe decided without further ado to join their ranks.

He completed his third airplane, a small tractor parasol-wing monoplane, in the fall of 1911 in the back of his brother Carlo's grocery store, every member of the family assisting in its construction. When it was completed, Bellanca took the craft to the flying field at Mineola where, before bemused habitués, he quietly assembled it with the stated intention of teaching himself to fly.

The fuselage consisted of just two longerons separated by vertical members. A seat precariously straddled the lower longeron, while a wire-braced wing sat above and ahead. The presence of a 30-hp Anzani engine kept the skeletal craft from looking like a primary glider, which in great measure it was, and tall angular surfaces sat atop the tail cone.

After assembling his plane in a rented shed, Bellanca began making straight hops in it. The craft flew easily a few feet above the ground, settling in gently when the throttle was retarded. In this manner, "Little Joe," as he was sometimes called, gained a feel for the controls. In response to the oft-quoted statement that God would have given man wings if he had wanted him to fly, Bellanca would reply that perhaps God had given him a brain to devise wings. He jokingly told friends that his first real flight would reveal if this were indeed so.

The day of this flight finally came. Bellanca was concerned that his muscular coordination in the strange art of flight might not be adequate, but his gentle bank passed without incident. Flying still higher, he completed one circle and then another before landing. When he came down, he found he was a member of a new fraternity, his fellow pilots crowding around to offer their congratulations. His plane was successful, he had taught himself how to fly, and in September 1912, he formed the Bellanca Aeroplane Company and Flying School to manufacture planes and use them in flight training.

The Bellanca Parasol had just one seat and a 30-hp Anzani engine which would spatter the pilot with oil. Students were taught to fly with the aid of a throttle limiter, which initially allowed only brief hops.

The pilot sat on a sort of a bird perch, wrote famous barnstorming pilot Clarence Chamberlin, *where he could look straight down and see nothing but thin air between him and the ground he had been rash enough to leave. It had a three-cylinder Anzani motor right in front of the pilot's face that could always be counted on to spatter the intrepid aviator with hot oil even if it did no worse to him. . . . I flew the thing myself at Roosevelt Field in 1921 after spending a lot of time replacing the original three-cylinder powerplant with a six-cylinder Anzani. It few all right but I thought I would never get it down, the wind was so high and it was so light. My curiosity was quite satisfied; I was thoroughly convinced that Bellanca not only was a genius but a hero of rare sort.*[2]

The system of instruction used by Bellanca was a simple one. He used a throttle limiter to allow initially just enough horsepower for his students to make brief hops, counseling them in their "grass cutting" as they learned the rudiments of control. He was unable to fly with them as the parasol monoplanes were too light to lift two. This activity continued through 1915 and approximately a dozen students were instructed per year. Two planes were reportedly used in the training, which was conducted first at Hempstead and later at the flying field near Garden City. Among those taught to fly personally by Giuseppe Bellanca was Fiorello H. LaGuardia, who achieved fame first as a bomber pilot and leader in World War I and then as the irrepressible mayor of New York City. LaGuardia had just purchased a Model T Ford (which he did not know how to handle) and offered to teach Bellanca to drive in return for flying lessons. The ride was nothing short of hilarious, both men arriving at the airport with the firm conviction that flying would be simple by comparison.

Contracted by the Maryland Pressed Steel Company, G. M. Bellanca designed the C.D., which first flew in 1916. It was a trim biplane with a wing span of twenty-six feet and an empty weight of just 400 pounds. Lateral control was accomplished through the use of wing warping instead of ailerons.

Caught up with the possibilities of the airplane, a company in Maryland contracted G. M. Bellanca to design for them a plane that could be mass-produced as a trainer. The result was a trim biplane that was powered by a 30-hp Anzani engine, had a wingspan of 26 feet, and weighed only 400 pounds empty. Completed in September 1916, the model C.D. first flew from Daub's Meadow, Maryland, now the athletic field of South Hagerstown High School. This plane was damaged by Bellanca in a fast landing at Brunswick, New Jersey. Flown again with an exuberant ex-military pilot at the controls, the C.D. once more sustained damage in landing. These mishaps notwithstanding, it proved to be quite a good plane during testing on Long Island by Arthur Heinrich during the first few months of 1917.

In his first flight in the C.D., Heinrich gave a dramatic demonstration of its inherent stability by releasing the controls 1,000 feet above the ground. With the throttle wide open it climbed straight ahead; when retarded to cruising power the plane flew straight and level. Finally, still with hands off the stick and feet off the rudder bar, Heinrich closed the throttle completely and the plane settled into a gentle glide.

The C.D. was in many ways a transition aircraft between the pre-World War I types and the configuration that would dominate aircraft design in the decade to follow. Like the Blériot, the C.D. used wing warping for lateral control instead of ailerons. It was a streamlined biplane with few bracing wires, however, and had a partially cowled radial engine and other aerodynamic considerations that gave it a top speed of 75 mph as opposed to the Blériot's 50.

The designer had in mind the idea of presenting a machine which would be popular for sport flying as well as training. The appeal of the C.D. in the latter role was limited, however, by a tiny front cockpit that seemed to be an afterthought in the design rather than a true second seat. It was in an effort to correct this shortcoming that the Maryland Pressed Steel Company brought out the Model C.E. in 1919.

The Bellanca C.E. was all that one could have wished for in an airplane. It featured ailerons instead of wing warping, a true front cockpit, and a 6-cylinder Anzani radial engine producing 45 to 55 hp. A very lovely little craft, the C.E. combined economy with surprisingly good performance. Initial rate of climb with pilot and passenger was 620 feet per minute, maximum speed was 102 mph, and landing speed was under 40 mph. Paul Stonebreaker, a Hagerstown native and veteran Army test pilot, made the initial flight evaluation of the C.E.

During World War I, large contracts were held by the Maryland Pressed Steel Company with the governments of Russia, France, and the United States for the production of 37-millimeter guns, carriages, and ammunition; 34-inch naval mines; and minesweeping equipment. With the coming of the Armistice in November 1918, these contracts were of course cancelled. Production of the C.E. had been delayed due to difficulties in obtaining Anzani engines from France, and the predictable postwar slump in aviation combined with the other troubles to force the Maryland Pressed Steel Company into receivership in 1920, after only two C.E. biplanes had been flown.

One of Bellanca's associates during his stay in Maryland was Lewis E. Reisner, a high school student born in Hagerstown a few months before the Wright brothers' historic powered flight late in 1903. After establishing himself as operator of Hagerstown's first airport, he became vice-president and general manager of the Kreider-Reisner Aircraft Company in 1927, and stayed on as vice-president when that company was absorbed by the Fairchild Aviation Corporation in 1929. Through Reisner, the Fairchild Republic Company (a division of Fairchild Industries which still manufactures aircraft in Hagerstown) can trace its history all the way back to the Bellanca C.D. of 1917.

The first C.E. had been purchased by Clarence Chamberlin, who had been a U.S. Army Air Service instructor in the First World War. *Fourteen months were to elapse before I finally got delivery of the machine*, he wrote, *and when I did it was equipped with a 45-horsepower motor in place of the stronger one originally specified. But instead of 102 miles an hour, it made 104! And it would carry with ease one person besides the pilot, whereas Army Jennies which all of us had flown had a high speed of something like 65 miles an hour, with a 90-horsepower motor, and would carry no more useful load. I was to find out frequently in my later acquaintance with Mr. Bellanca that, unlike many designers, his estimates usually were conservative about what his ships would do, rather than over-optimistic.*[3]

Chamberlin was extremely impressed with the Sicilian-born designer, whom he found to be quiet and earnest. They became friends instantly although neither sensed the roles they were to play in each other's fortunes. That their names would be household words seven years later would undoubtedly have surprised both of them greatly.

The C.E. turned out to be a wonderful barnstorming airplane, Chamberlin using it with great success in Maryland, Pennsylvania, New Jersey, and New York. *My rates were $15 a hop for straight flying*, he recalled in *Record Flights*, his autobiography, *and $25 a ride if the passenger wanted to 'get the works.' Most of them preferred stunt flights, first, because they wanted to get a 'real thrill,' and secondly, because it soon became apparent that my little Bellanca plane did a lot more things than the other barnstorming planes which were war surplus stock and quite clumsy by comparison. Even those who had been up before were frequently enticed by the swiftness and 'maneuverability' of my ship into spending their money for another ride.*[4]

The high regard of this former Army pilot for the graceful biplanes led him to buy up the remaining partially completed C.E.s at auction prices after Maryland Pressed Steel closed its doors. Sadly, not one Bellanca C.E. remains in existence.

That Giuseppe M. Bellanca was already held in high regard as a designer of airplanes was evidenced by the fact that the rudder of the C.E. bore his name in large black lettering, while the name of the manufacturer appeared only in small print in the circular emblem below. It is not surprising, therefore, that Bellanca was approached in 1921 by a group of men anxious to bring aviation to Omaha, Nebraska.

The Bellanca C.E. of 1919 was an excellent trainer, offering more room than the C.D. and featuring ailerons.

"Professor" Bellanca, as he was often admiringly called by his associates, had hoped to obtain $50,000 for the construction and marketing of a new concept he envisioned in aircraft design. T. Richards and Reed Davis, on the other hand, were only able to offer $7,000 in capital, but Bellanca accepted this as times were difficult in the young aviation industry and slim pickings were better than none. An agreement was signed between the designer and the North Platte Aircraft Company on April 29, 1921, calling for the development of one aircraft to specifications proposed by Bellanca, who was to be paid $390 per month. That volume production of the new plane, designated the C.F., was planned is evident in the original contract, which called for the company "to buy . . . fifty new Anzani ninety-five horsepower motors, which can be purchased for $375 each, at this time, and the cost of said motors, the first party agrees to finance."[5]

Bellanca arrived in Nebraska in the summer of 1921, accompanied by his friend and helper Pietro Marullo. After six months, with construction of the plane well under way, the company ran out of money. Bellanca never received the salary promised him and had to put up with the sweltering heat of July and the bitter cold of January far from the comfort of his home in Brooklyn.

Among the potential investors the aircraft designer approached was a wealthy farmer who, having given his wholehearted promise of financial support, would each time go away only to return skeptical and have to be convinced all over again. The source of this vacillation turned out to be his wife, who felt aviation to be an unwise investment at best. With each successive promise of support the farmer would wave aside the matter of payment with the ambiguous comment "in due time and fair season," a phrase G. M. Bellanca would recall humorously in the years to follow.

The solution to the problem of finances was not long in coming, although it still represented considerably less money than Bellanca had wished to obtain. An Omaha motorcycle dealer named Victor H. Roos felt that aviation would be a propitious area of endeavor and, with A. H. Fetters of the Union Pacific Railroad and several others, formed the Roos-Bellanca Aircraft Company to undertake the completion and marketing of the C.F. The designer was now free to proceed with the task of building the plane by hand, a situation not altered in any way by his being named as one of the organization's three directors.

Under the new arrangement, work was transferred to the rear of a firehouse, where the small team was joined by a young woman named Dorothy Brown. The daughter of an Omaha restauranteur who owned the building in which Bellanca had taken temporary lodgings, Dorothy acted as secretary, traced aircraft drawings, and even lent a hand at times in the mysterious process of constructing an airplane. The Sicilian-born aircraft designer and the first-generation American of British descent fell in love, Bellanca selling one of two surplus engines he possessed in order to buy her a small diamond ring. Taking time off from the project, something heretofore not even considered by Giuseppe, turned out not to be a simple matter under the stern management of company president Victor Roos, even though the request came from a fellow officer in the firm and the guiding genius behind the entire undertaking. For their honeymoon, Roos gave the Bellancas an entire afternoon off.

The mundane considerations of domesticity intruded themselves on the sublime work in progress on other occasions as well. At one point, Bellanca sent woodworker Pietro Marullo home for a vitally needed part only to wait in vain for his return. A search was initiated and Marullo was found to be in a

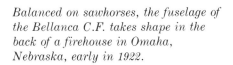

Balanced on sawhorses, the fuselage of the Bellanca C.F. takes shape in the back of a firehouse in Omaha, Nebraska, early in 1922.

20

The lifting strut, a supporting member with an airfoil contour, was a unique feature of Bellanca cabin monoplanes. One of the struts for the C.F., photographed before being covered with fabric and installed on the plane, shows the two-spar structure. Balsa wood was used in the leading edge to keep weight to a minimum. (Courtesy John Underwood)

Just completed, the Bellanca C.F. sits in an open field in the summer of 1922. Typical of the period, the plane was fitted with a nonsteerable tail skid instead of a tail wheel and was not intended for use on a modern runway. (Courtesy Theron Rinehart/Fairchild Republic Company)

The C.F. is streamlined, with few protrusions to increase aerodynamic drag. An exception is the cylinders of the engine, which are exposed for cooling.

local grocery store. His wife had put her foot down, demanding in a dire ultimatum that Marullo do the shopping before dinnertime. Despite such interruptions, the monoplane took shape and was finished after a year of long days and weekends sacrificed to the project.

As already mentioned, the C.F. was designed with an open cockpit behind the passenger cabin. The humped back of its airfoil-shaped fuselage blocked virtually all forward visibility, although the cockpit was offset to the left so that the pilot could lean out and look forward under the left wing. This was, of course, a less satisfactory configuration than placing the pilot in front of the passengers in the enclosed cabin, where he could enjoy an excellent field of view and shelter from the rain. Aviation was in its robust and adventurous youth, however, and Giuseppe Bellanca knew well that the aviators of the day would be loath to give up the psychological freedom of the open cockpit.

Giuseppe Bellanca stands before the Bellanca C.F. (Courtesy Dr. William L. Stearman)

The C.F. had a wing span of 40 feet and was 23 feet 10 inches in length. The use of clear instead of pigmented dope to tauten the fabric may have been dictated by economic considerations, but the absence of bright colors instead conveyed a refined elegance. The plane was an unembellished expression of the beliefs and talents of the designer. Completed with Bellanca's remaining surplus engine under the constraints of a limited budget, and lacking all but the most rudimentary instrumentation, the craft nevertheless seemed to exude luxury. Built with hope, pride, and excellent craftsmanship, buffed and resplendent as a new carriage, the Bellanca C.F. was wheeled out into the sunshine early in June 1922.

The Amazing Bellanca Monoplane

Harry G. Smith, a thirty-one-year-old airmail pilot, flew the Bellanca C.F. on its first flight, which took place on June 8, 1922.

It was my privilege to give the Bellanca its first 'hop', wrote Harry G. Smith, a thirty-one-year-old airmail pilot based in Omaha, Nebraska. *The ease with which the plane is handled is extraordinary. . . . It is quite sensitive on the controls and yet not over sensitive. . . . In fact it is the most correctly balanced and easiest handled plane I ever flew.*

That the plane was indeed in perfect trim was evidenced by the fact that after its initial twenty hours in the air, all flown by Smith, no realignment of any component was necessary. *The plane has a rare combination of stability and maneuverability,* the pilot observed. *On several occasions I flew it six or eight complete circles in a bank of about 30 degrees with hands off the stick, controlling the plane entirely with the rudder. With the throttle at a cruising position the plane will fly hands-off without gaining or losing altitude. Open the throttle a little and the plane will slightly nose up and begin to climb. Close the throttle entirely and the plane will take a good normal gliding position. Together with this stability is a remarkable maneuverability. This plane will out maneuver planes of even more horsepower. With the greatest ease it will loop, roll, and wing-over. It goes into a spin with some difficulty and comes out extremely easy.*

On June 10, 1922, two days after its first flight, the C.F. was flown to Fort Crook, Nebraska, where it was officially clocked in speed trials by the U.S. Army. Averaging the results obtained by observers with flags and stopwatches as the plane made six passes overhead—three in each direction to negate the effects of any wind—produced an official top speed of 109.8 miles per hour. As for flight characteristics, Smith declared that the C.F. handled

As a concession to World War I pilots, who were accustomed to open cockpits, the pilot of the C.F. was positioned behind the passenger cabin instead of inside it. To compensate for the total lack of forward visibility over the airfoil-shaped fuselage, the cockpit was offset to the left to allow the pilot to lean out and look under the left wing. (Ernest Bihler Collection via John Underwood)

This photograph, taken sixty years ago, is the only known view of the Bellanca C.F. in flight. Although the quality of this view is poor, it serves to show the handsome lines of the cabin monoplane.

The simplicity of the structure of the C.F. is evident in the tail. An aero-dynamically balanced rudder is mounted directly on the fuselage, a feature common to many World War I-era aircraft. Although there is no vertical stabilizer above the horizontal surfaces, there is a fixed vertical surface underneath to round out the shape of the rudder. (Courtesy John Underwood)

A view from the right side well illustrates the exceptionally clean lines of the C.F. With power off, the plane had a glide ratio of more than 12:1. In the event of an engine failure a mile above the ground, the monoplane could fly twelve miles before having to land, a feature that added to its great safety. (Courtesy John Underwood)

like a military fighter but with a more uniform and accurate response. "If this machine had dual controls," he stated, "I feel that I could teach anyone to fly in one week."[6]

A week to the day after its first flight, the C.F. entered the Midwestern Flying Meet at Monmouth, Illinois. Flying directly from Fort Crook by way of Des Moines, Iowa, a distance of three hundred miles, took the cabin monoplane five hours and eleven minutes against a moderate headwind. Total fuel consumption was 21½ gallons, which averaged out to 14 miles per gallon, despite the headwind.

All four events in the meet were swept by the Bellanca. It won the speed contest, flying the 15-mile triangular circuit in 9 minutes 30 seconds to beat the next best time of 11 minutes 30 seconds set by the very pretty Oriole biplane built by Curtiss. In the event to determine climbing ability, the C.F. reached 7,000 feet in just 11 minutes, while the Oriole with its 160-hp Hispano-Suiza engine put in an even poorer showing, managing to stagger up to 5,600 feet in 12½ minutes. Perhaps the best test of efficiency was the gliding event in which competing aircraft had to shut off their engines at 2,000 feet and remain aloft as long as possible. The Bellanca C.F. won this contest with a time of 4 minutes 43 seconds, demonstrating an excellent glide ratio of 12:1, while the airplane taking second place—the Laird Swallow biplane with a 90-hp Curtiss OX-5 engine—came down in 3 minutes 44 seconds.

To say that the cabin monoplane caused a sensation scarcely conveys the excitement that must have been felt when, with just 90 hp to propel its capacious airframe, the C.F. emerged victorious after three days of competition. It was awarded five silver cups, four for the individual events and a fifth for winning them all. Pictures of the C.F., bearing the race number 22 in chalk on the fuselage, began appearing in the aeronautical publications of the day.

William C. Hopson, then the third-ranking pilot in the U.S. Air Mail Service, took over flying the Bellanca after the Monmouth meet. *When I went out to take my initial hop in the Bellanca,* he wrote, *I was in a skeptical mood with eyes open for defects and faults rather than good qualities. My first ride lasted forty-five minutes during which time I put her through her paces. I went up a skeptic but came down a firm believer in the Bellanca C.F. She was by far the most remarkable performing plane I had ever flown or dreamed of*

Victor Roos, a motorcycle dealer in Omaha, provided financial backing for the completion of the C.F. With pleasure evident in their expressions, Roos and G. M. Bellanca shake hands in front of first-place trophies won by the C.F. at the Midwestern Flying Meet at Monmouth, Illinois, just a week after its first flight. (Courtesy John Underwood)

Veteran airmail pilot William C. Hopson took over the flying of the C.F. and won first place in every event entered in two additional air meets in 1922.

flying. Since that time I have flown her about forty hours and each flight has strengthened my belief in this plane. For climb, speed, gliding, weight carrying, and ease of operation under all conditions of practical flying, she is years ahead of any plane in the world today.[7]

Hopson took the C.F. to the Tarkio Aero Meet which was held on July 27, 28, and 29, 1922, in Tarkio, Missouri. The businessmen of this progressive community, a college town of three thousand inhabitants, hoped to stimulate tourism through the thrilling spectacle of a large-scale air show. All comers were invited to compete for silver cups and cash prizes, to be awarded after each of the four individual events comprising the meet. To ensure a good turnout of entrants, the sponsors also agreed to pay the expenses of gas, oil, and hotel accomodations for the pilots, as well as provide entertainment. The site of the competition was an eighty-acre bluegrass field adjacent to the town.

The Bellanca C.F. once again took first place in every event. *In the climbing contest at Tarkio,* Hopson wrote, *I arrived at 2,000 feet altitude in two minutes when a Fokker who was the nearest competitor was at 1,700 feet. In the gliding contest, I remained in the air for five minutes and twenty seconds after shutting off all power at 2,000 feet.*

Hopson continued to pile up flying time in the C.F. after the Tarkio Aero Meet. His enthusiasm was great when he took the plane to the Interstate Aero Meet at Norfolk, Nebraska, another three-day competition beginning

Two aerial marriages were performed in the Bellanca C.F. in August 1922. From left to right in the second wedding party are a bystander, Victor Roos, best man Herman Tappert, bridegroom Fred Hoffman, bride Esther Comfert, Judge T. V. Norvell, and G. M. Bellanca. In addition to providing unusual entertainment at an air meet, these marriages graphically illustrated the advantages of a monoplane with an enclosed cabin and seating for four. (Courtesy John Underwood)

Right:
With the champion aircraft as a backdrop, Bellanca and Roos proudly display the grand-prize trophy at the conclusion of the Norfolk Meet. At this time, the C.F. had won thirteen first-place awards in just ten weeks. (Courtesy John Underwood)

Roos and Hopson stand on either side of the first-place trophies won by the Bellanca C.F. at Tarkio, Missouri, in late July 1922. (Courtesy John Underwood)

August 24, 1922. For the third time in a row, the monoplane designed by Giuseppe Bellanca placed first in every event in which it participated.

At Norfolk, the pilot observed, the official time for the Bellanca in a speed contest over a three-point course, three laps of ten miles each, was 109 mph. This speed was made with a Jenny prop of only five foot pitch, having broken our regular propeller of seven foot eleven inch pitch with which I made unofficial speed of 115 mph.

An interesting sidelight of the show was the use of the Bellanca C.F. to conduct two aerial marriages. These weddings were tremendously popular with the crowd and received a fair amount of attention from the regional newspapers as well. "With the bride and groom, minister and best man," Hopson wrote, "I left the ground after a run of just two hundred feet against practically no headwind."

These poetic marriages above the earth, appearing to be little more than sensational stunts, in fact reflected the desire of Victor Roos to impress upon the public the advantages of a cabin monoplane. A wedding requires room for four people seated in such a way that the ceremony can actually be performed. The Laird Swallow, typical of the airplanes against which the C.F. competed at Norfolk, paled by comparison to the Bellanca since its well-appointed but noisy front cockpit could accomodate only two passengers.

Few present at the meet doubted that the C.F. represented the wave of the future in aerial transportation. Passengers could board and exit with relative ease, there being no bottom wing to clamber over. If the cabin monoplane were to find a market so that it could be built and sold in large numbers, then it was critical that the public be aware of and accept the difference between this configuration and all others.

The cabin was made for comfort, Harry Smith proclaimed. *It is as large and roomy as an ordinary four-passenger enclosed automobile. There is ample room for four passengers to be seated comfortably and with plenty of leg room. The door is large enough for easy entrance and exit.*

Bill Hopson agreed with his fellow airmail pilot. *The cabin of the Bellanca is roomy and comfortably seats four passengers, and the noise has been reduced so that it is possible for the pilot to talk to the passengers who are at least four feet ahead.*

Aviation was just entering its golden years, although it was still a summer pursuit to air-minded America. With the approach of autumn came the end of the air-show season, and the champion monoplane was allowed for the time being to rest on its laurels. Hopson was well satisfied with the two shows in which he had flown, writing: *We entered contests competing with the best planes in the country with motors more than double and triple the motor used in the Bellanca. I won seven first prizes in these two meets, each contest being virtually a walk-away.*

The designer was the most pleased of all, although his modesty prevented him from stepping into the limelight he so richly deserved. Instead he beamed his huge smile even more than usual, his brown eyes twinkling. In his papers he noted the fact that the C.F., with a heavy 90-hp engine purchased from the Army for $35, had bettered both a Breguet and a Fokker, these aircraft each having 400 hp at their disposal. Thirteen trophies had been won in ten weeks without a single second-place showing to mar the string of firsts.

With this impressive record in hand, Victor H. Roos began a program to tap the market he felt existed for an airplane such as the C.F. A thirty-four-year-old business-college graduate fascinated with aviation, Roos saw to it that prestigious aviation journals in the United States, England, and France were provided with data and photographs. In addition, he had Air Mail Service pilots Smith and Hopson put down their impressions in typed, legal-sized, one-page documents beginning "TO WHOM IT MAY CONCERN." Every avenue was explored in the hope that somewhere a need for the plane would be perceived.

It seems difficult to believe that the Bellanca C.F. was not an immediate success. There is always a lag between technological advancement and public acceptance, however, and it was to be another five summers before Captain Charles Augustus Lindbergh would plunge America—and the world—whole-heartedly into the air age with his crossing of the Atlantic in the Ryan NYP *Spirit of St. Louis*. The C.F. did not go unnoticed, though, in part due to

G. M. Bellanca avoided the limelight, being quiet and somewhat shy. His famous smile speaks for him, nevertheless, in this photograph taken after the Monmouth Meet. (Courtesy John Underwood)

Wearing race number 12, the C.F. participated in the thrilling National Air Races of 1923, the nation's largest air meet. The spinner has been removed in this photograph of the plane taxiing in. The severely restricted forward visibility of the pilot is evident. (Courtesy John Underwood)

Declared the winner in both speed and efficiency in the arduous Aviation Country Club of Detroit Competition, the C.F. easily beat the highly rated Curtiss Oriole and Laird Swallow. (Courtesy U.S. Air Force)

Roos's efforts, and in some measure also thanks to the British publication *Jane's All the World's Aircraft*. This definitive source on aviation development around the world singled out the Bellanca cabin monoplane in its 1923 edition as "the first up-to-date transport aeroplane that was designed, built, and flown with success in the United States."[8]

Prior to precedent-setting antitrust rulings in 1934, it was a common practice for a single company to produce airplanes and then operate them itself as airliners. Such a venture was the reason for a reorganization of the Roos-Bellanca Airplane company early in 1923. The president of the new concern was Myles Standish, a manufacturer of automotive parts and accessories who provided much of the backing. Victor Roos became vice-president and G. M. Bellanca was retained as consulting engineer at $90 a week. This decade in American history was one in which commercial aviation operations consisted almost exclusively of carrying the mails, however, as not enough revenue could be generated transporting the small trickle of passengers that might be expected. (Even the Ford Tri-Motor of 1927 was incapable of making a profit without a government airmail subsidy, the Douglas DC-3 of 1936 being the first airliner able to pay its way just by hauling passengers.) It is therefore not surprising that none of the dozen Bellanca C.F. "airliners" was built.

Although his hopes for commercial manufacture of the C.F. remained high, Giuseppe Bellanca was already branching out in different areas. At the beginning of the year he initiated negotiations with the U.S. Postal Service to develop new wings for their antiquated de Havilland DH-4 mail planes. On paper there existed the C.G., an improved C.F. with either a Curtiss OX-5 (which could scarcely be called an improvement) or an Hispano-Suiza engine. In his mind was the idea for a much more advanced cabin monoplane which would bring him fame.

In the fall of 1923 came the thrilling National Air Races, bombastically hailed also as the International Air Races in the press and official programs, a nine-event extravaganza of the newest, fastest, and finest airplanes the country could produce. Among the two events scheduled for Friday, October 5, the second day of the races, was the Aviation Country Club of Detroit Trophy competition for light commercial aircraft, and the Bellanca C.F. appeared among the entrants sporting race number 12. The year before had seen only three airplanes entered, one being a poorly disguised military craft of dubious commercial value, but this year the lineup at Lambert Field in St. Louis, Missouri, promised a more satisfying competition.

Eight planes had entered. The new Berliner monoplane, which was to have been flown by Edmund T. Allen—later the famous Boeing test pilot—was withdrawn by telegram. The seven ships that did participate were the Bellanca, the Laird Swallow, the Curtiss Oriole, the Raco (the old Orenco Tourister, renamed by the Robertson Aircraft Company), the Le Père, the Standard U-1 Special (also entered by the Robertson Aircraft Company), and the Huff-Daland Petrel Model 4.

The race consisted of five laps around a 50-kilometer (31-mile) course, with $500, $300, and $200 to be awarded the first-, second-, and third-place winners in each of the two categories of speed and efficiency. The race began at eleven o'clock, strong winds making for less than ideal conditions. Army Lieutenant Harold R. Harris, the winner the year before at a fast 134.9 mph, was the first to experience trouble. The failure of bearings in the timing gear of his 180-hp Wright E engine forced him out on the first lap, but he successfully landed the Huff-Daland on a rough part of the field.

The Standard and Le Pere both dropped out in the third lap, the latter crashing without serious injury to pilot J. L. Burns. A bearing in his geared

Another photograph of the C.F. taken at the National Air Races of 1923 shows that the individual curved stacks were removed and an exhaust collector ring was added. (Courtesy August T. Bellanca)

The Laird Swallow was a very good sport biplane. Looking somewhat like a smaller, newer Curtiss Jenny, it was powered by an OX-5 engine and could carry two passengers in addition to the pilot.

The Swallow, the Oriole, and the C.F. were powered by engines of equal power. It is a remarkable tribute to G. M. Bellanca's genius, therefore, that his plane won so easily, since it had to carry ballast approximating the weight of two additional passengers. (Courtesy Walter J. Addems)

Charles S. "Casey" Jones, the well-known Curtiss demonstration pilot, became a familiar sight on the air-race circuit in his modified Curtiss Oriole biplane.

210-hp Hispano-Suiza engine had burned out, causing the powerplant to seize. In the Standard, Frank Robertson—one day away from his twenty-eighth birthday—made a successful emergency landing when water in the fuel supply caused the 150-hp Hisso to quit. A similar fate befell his older brother, who was in the Raco, a biplane powered by a 150-hp Hispano-Suiza. Trained as military pilots in World War I, the brothers operated a flight school and aircraft company in St. Louis, and flew the mail. One young pilot they hired for their St. Louis-to-Chicago route was Charles Lindbergh, and they would be among the first to back him in his effort to fly the Atlantic.

With four planes down, the race was ironically left to the three lowest-powered entrants. The Oriole and Swallow biplanes, both equipped with Curtiss OX-5 engines with a rated horsepower identical to the Bellanca's Anzani, were unable to match the performance of the C.F., despite the fact that it had to carry more ballast due to the greater number of seats. C. S. "Casey" Jones, the famous Curtiss demonstration pilot, came in third with an elapsed time of 113 minutes in the company's Oriole; Perry Hutton placed second at 107 minutes in the Laird Swallow sponsored by the Sterling Oil and Refining Company; and L. H. "Jack" Atkinson took first-place honors in the now-veteran C.F. The standing was also the same for efficiency, the Bellanca having a figure of merit of 674.8 as opposed to 300.4 and 285.6 for the Swallow and Oriole respectively. (These figures were determined by dividing the gross weight of the plane, at which it was required to race, by the total horsepower of the engine, and multiplying the result by the average speed attained in miles per hour.)

The poor showing by the two biplanes would suggest that they were not very good aircraft. In fact, they were highly regarded by the aviation community, and as successful as one could hope in view of the postwar slump in aviation as a whole. The Oriole and the Swallow were products of proven design techniques, newer and somewhat better than those aircraft they replaced. While they represented the end of the line of development that was perhaps best typified by the Curtiss JN-4, the C.F. marked the emergence of a new line that would make leather helmets and goggles things of the past.

The Bellanca, the Jenny, and the Jacuzzi

An understanding of the significance of the Bellanca C.F. Cabin Monoplane may be gained by studying its efficiency in relation to its contemporaries. The unique position of this airplane against the background of aviation history in the United States will help the reader to draw conclusions regarding its relative importance.

Aircraft design has always been a science of compromise. Top speed may be increased, but often at the expense of range due to the use of a more powerful engine with higher fuel consumption, and utility may suffer since a heavier engine means less carrying capability when the increased empty weight is subtracted from the gross weight. A higher wing loading may be selected to improve the speed of a plane, but the stall speed will also rise and the ability to

The Curtiss JN-4 Jenny was one of the most significant aircraft in American aviation.

get into and out of small fields will be impaired. Weight is critical in an airplane, leading to the famous design maxim "Simplicate and add lightness," and no change in any one area of design can be expected not to have an effect somewhere else. One may conclude, therefore, that no direct comparison of performance and specifications among aircraft will necessarily be very revealing.

The task of comparison is facilitated if we choose aircraft of identical horsepower and similar overall weight. In this regard we are lucky, for the Curtiss JN-4 Jenny matches very closely. It is the plane that dominated the aviation scene in this country, was available as surplus by the thousand, and kept newer types from finding a market since they were unable to compete with a price tag often as low as $250.

The ten-cylinder Anzani radial powerplant of the Bellanca and the eight-cylinder Curtiss engine of the Jenny both weighed around 400 pounds and were rated at 90 hp. If the OX-5 is affectionately remembered for never turning out its full horsepower, the same might be said of the Anzani, which was produced in France and Britain. At one air meet, a famous French aviator asked G. M. Bellanca how many horsepower his C.F. had. Upon hearing the reply he threw up his hands and exclaimed: "You do not even have ninety donkeys!"

The comparison of aircraft weights holds some surprises. Although one would be likely to guess that the five-passenger Bellanca weighed more than the two-seat, open-cockpit Jenny, the opposite is in fact true. The gross weight of the C.F. is 1,990 pounds, while the figure for the Curtiss trainer is 2,130 pounds. A greater surprise comes when one examines the empty weights of each plane; without fuel, oil, or passengers, the Jenny weighs 1,580 pounds, and the Bellanca tips the scales at only 950 pounds! Against a useful load of 550 pounds for the trainer, the cabin monoplane offers a useful load of 1,040 pounds.

For a plane to be able to lift more than its own weight was indeed rare. *The first flight that was made with a load,* Harry G. Smith wrote, *I made with 625 pounds of sand in the cabin. The plane took this load off very easily and I am convinced that it will carry, in addition to the weight of the pilot and full fuel capacity, 700 or 750 pounds of payload. With a full load the speed of the plane seems to be practically the same as when empty and it handles with the same ease, the balance remaining the same.*[9]

William G. Hopson also commented on this aspect of the aircraft's performance. *Although the owners of this plane have been very conservative about weight carrying,* he stated, *the actual payload carried being 650 pounds besides the pilot, I firmly believe that this plane will successfully fly with a payload of 1,000 pounds. With a payload of 550 pounds I have maintained a horizontal flight with five cylinders shut off, using only about 35 hp.*[10] *Although this plane is very light, it is exceptionally strong and will handle very nicely both in the air and during landing and takeoff in very heavy adverse wind conditions. She can be taken off and landed in very small fields and with her remarkable climbing ability will get over high obstructions at the edge of the field.*[11]

Initial rate-of-climb of the Bellanca C.F. was 1,100 feet per minute if the pilot alone were aboard. With five people and full fuel, that figure dropped to a still respectable 600 feet per minute. The Curtiss JN-4, on the other hand, could barely stagger off the ground on hot days. If the pilot were giving a heavy friend a ride, he would have to take off in a direction where there were no hills, steeples, or other obstructions, for while the biplane would break ground quickly, it would take forever to gain any altitude. The ceiling of the

W. S. Henson devised the "Aerial Steam Carriage" in 1843. A fanciful rendering based on the work of Sir George Cayley, the image of this flying carriage was published constantly for more than half a century and accustomed the public to the general arrangement of the aeroplane. In configuration, the "Aerial Steam Carriage" is a high-wing monoplane with an enclosed cabin.

OX-5-powered Jenny was little more than 6,000 feet, and however nostalgic former JN-4 pilots might be, they will heartily agree that the more powerful Hispano-Suiza engine made the trainer a far better aircraft.

These observations are in no way intended to be a criticism of the Curtiss JN-4, which is one of the most famous airplanes in the history of American aviation. It was indeed a good trainer, and anyone who mastered it could fly anything with wings. In flight it was marginally unstable, but so well damped that things went wrong slowly enough for the novice pilot to keep on top of them. Having to grease the exposed rocker arms of the Curtiss OX-5 after each flight taught him to be continually aware of his engine, and knowing it could and would quit at any time taught him to be continually aware of potential landing fields below. The Curtiss Jenny did not pale by the standards of 1922; it set them.

That these two aircraft of the same power and gross weight had such disparate performances is a tribute to G. M. Bellanca. That his creation also carried five people instead of two is astounding. Even sixty years later, with the benefit of technological advancement, the performance of the Bellanca C.F. remains remarkable.

The C.F. is significant for what it was rather than for what it did, despite its popularity as an air-show veteran. It was the prototype of the first line of successful cabin monoplanes in the United States, all its famous successors inheriting a legacy of unmatched efficiency. The cabin monoplane concept, as has already been stated, is virtually as old as the idea of the airplane itself, and may be traced directly to the Henson Aerial Steam Carriage of 1846. Before the histories of the *Columbia* and other record-setting Bellancas of the late twenties and thirties are presented, more must be said about the importance of an enclosed cabin in the development of aviation.

The extravagance of an enclosed compartment for pilot and crew was one that the early pioneers could ill afford. The Wright 1903 Flyer had just twelve horsepower to propel its weight of six hundred pounds, and flew so slowly that the slipstream was hardly a problem. Poetic images of aerial carriages aside, the builder of early aeroplanes had to be practical. Planes were frameworks, just as Otto Lilienthal's hang gliders had been, and weight was a critical factor.

A partially enclosed cockpit came about fairly quickly, but for good visibility and safety in the event the pilot had to scramble free on the ground—or jump from his plane if he were in the air—the top was left open.[12] The wind on his cheek during a side slip, the rush of the slipstream in the flying wires, and the direct roar of the engine, were all cues the early aviator would have been loath to give up.

After the initial invention and demonstration of the airplane in the United States, dominance in this new field of human endeavor shifted to Europe, where the potential of a flying machine as an instrument of warfare was early perceived. Initially employed for observation, aircraft improved rapidly in structural strength and performance during World War I, becoming rugged dogfighters and potent ground-attack weapons in a few short years.

Germany remained in the forefront of this technological boom, pioneering the construction of all-metal low-wing monoplanes with fully cantilevered wings. This very advanced technology carried over into peacetime with the appearance in 1919 of the revolutionary Junkers F 13. The significance of this plane cannot be overstated, for it was pressed into service in all parts of the world as the first airliner of modern configuration.

Although less famous, the Junkers K 16 and the Fokker F II/F III series were also cabin monoplanes used as airliners immediately after the First

Far ahead of its time, the Junkers F 13 was a low wing, all-metal monoplane transport with a completely enclosed passenger cabin. The engine was fully cowled and pilot and copilot sat in the logical position, ahead of the passengers. It was this plane more than any other that firmly established German leadership of the aviation industry in the years following World War I. (Courtesy Lufthansa)

The Junkers K 16 was another all-metal cabin monoplane used as an airliner just after World War I. (Courtesy Lufthansa)

World War. The Fokker, a larger development of the concepts embodied in the D VIII parasol fighter of 1918, was designed by Reinhold Platz and had a plywood-skinned wooden wing atop a fabric-cover steel tube fuselage. Developments of this line were to have a great influence on aviation in the United States. The two F IV transports built were purchased by the U.S. Army Air Service, one designated the T-2 becoming the first aircraft to fly nonstop across the American continent in 1923, while the later Fokker Trimotors played a variety of important roles.

The emergence of the cabin monoplane in the United States was not a happy affair. While aircraft of this configuration were being operated by Lufthansa, KLM, and other airlines on routes ranging across Europe, only one American plane with a single wing and an enclosed passenger compartment appeared in *Jane's All the World's Aircraft* prior to the Bellanca C.F. One of the sorrier craft to take to the sky, it was called the Jacuzzi.

Built by the Jacuzzi brothers of Berkeley, California, this seven-seat aircraft had a wing span of fifty-two feet and was powered by a 210-hp Hall-Scott L-6 engine. First flown late in 1920, the plane was intended to be used commercially. The window line was low under the wing, and the engine further blocked the view of the pilot, who sat inside with the passengers rather than in an open cockpit as was the case with the C.F. Even to the untrained eye the structural strength of the Jacuzzi looked questionable, but the builder pointed out that it had successfully penetrated extremely rough air over the Hayward Hills on a flight to Oakland, thereby proving itself to be sufficiently robust.

The Jacuzzi Monoplane crashed on the morning of July 14, 1921, while en route from the Yosemite Valley to San Francisco. *It seemed to be flying straight west and all of a sudden the left wing folded back*, stated an Air Service sergeant who was an eyewitness. *At first it appeared like a man throwing out hand bills, which I suppose was caused from the breaking of the struts and bracings and torn linen. The left wing left the ship entirely. The ship took a steep glide and what was peculiar to me was that it held that glide not flopping or twisting as one would expect it to do having lost one wing. At*

Perhaps the first true enclosed cabin monoplane to be built and flown in America, the Jacuzzi suffered from poor visibility and a lack of engineering acumen in its design.

A closeup of the Jacuzzi with the wings removed shows details of the interior, landing gear, and engine placement.

about 2,000 feet the right wing broke and left the ship very much in the same manner as the left wing, the fuselage continuing in its straight glide.[13]

A detailed examination was made of the wreckage in an attempt to understand why the plane had come apart in level flight through still air. There had been no fire, so the investigators had little difficulty in ascertaining that the main wing spars had cracked and broken near the fuselage attachment points. A superficial design analysis by Air Service engineers revealed the design of the monoplane to be dangerously deficient in three areas. First, the wing struts seemed improperly proportioned to take the torsional loads of so large a wing. Second, the axle of the landing gear was not set in the V formed by the gear legs. Thirdly, the use of a door running from the top to the bottom of the cabin side was thought to compromise the structural integrity of the fuselage.

At higher speeds, when the center of pressure was well back on the wing, torsional loads combined with normal flight loads to snap the wing struts in the middle. This is what had destroyed the plane, a creation of unsound engineering and construction practices. "This wreck clearly shows the necessity of technical control of all airplane construction," concluded investigator First Lieutenant Frank D. Hackett of Mather Field, "especially that which does not follow well tested and extensively used design."[14]

An additional unsafe feature, initially thought responsible for the crash, was the drilling-out of the steel bolts attaching the wing struts to the landing gear during a postproduction program for weight reduction. These bolts merely represented one element, however, in what was obviously a flying catastrophe. It had been the intent of the builders to form a regional airline using Jacuzzi monoplanes between Sacramento, Richmond, Oakland, and San Francisco, but the lack of basic engineering skill in the inception of the plane

The New Standard D-25, which appeared in 1929, was a five-seat biplane powered by a 220-hp Wright J5 Whirlwind engine. Intended for carrying passengers at low cost, it nevertheless needed more than twice the horsepower of the Bellanca C.F. to offer comparable performance.

A truly significant airplane in the development of aviation was the Northrop Alpha of 1929. Among the major advances in this all-metal design were the multicellular wing, stressed-skin semimonocoque fuselage, and full NACA cowling. Like the Bellanca C.F., it nevertheless retained the awkward rear placement of the open cockpit rather than placing the pilot in an enclosed cockpit at the front, where he would enjoy better visibility and protection from the weather. (Courtesy Warren M. Bodie)

doomed such plans and relegated the Jacuzzi to obscurity in American aviation history.

At the time of the crash, G. M. Bellanca was filling page after page of graph paper with lengthy calculations, observations, and metric notations in a neat Italian script. The contrast to the Jacuzzi could not have been greater; there would be no guesswork in the cabin monoplane designed by the "Professor."

It was the Curtiss Jenny, however, that was to have the last laugh. Many thousands had been built, and surplus stocks early in the decade after World War I seemed inexhaustible. The C.F. was certainly superior to the Jenny in every regard, but performance was sadly not at issue. With Curtiss JN-4s and Standard J-1s selling for as little as $250, a cabin monoplane costing $5,000 simply could not compete. Indignant at having been reminded of her age, Jenny quietly took her revenge on the Omaha group. As a result, no market would be found and only one Bellanca C.F. would be built. The subsequent history of this airplane will be detailed later in this book.

Turning Point:
The Wright Bellancas

Only a few de Havilland DH-4 mail planes were fitted with the new wings designed and built by G. M. Bellanca. Despite a significantly lower stall speed, and increased cruise speed and load-carrying ability, no additional orders were forthcoming from the Post Office Department.

GM. Bellanca could not help but be interested in the aviation activity around him in Omaha, a major hub in the young airmail system. Early in 1923, the Air Mail Service awarded contracts to several manufacturers for the development of new aircraft which could replace its fleet of converted wartime de Havilland bombers. With the construction of the C.F. now behind him, Ballanca had time to follow up an idea which had been forming in the back of his mind.

Night flights were soon to be undertaken in addition to daytime operations, and the Air Mail Service was especially anxious to provide its pilots with every advantage possible. Knowing this, the designer asked to be allowed to design and build a new set of wings for the DH-4 that would substantially reduce operating costs and increase safety.

New wings for de Havilland mail planes had been tried before, but with only limited success, and the Service was skeptical of Giuseppe Bellanca's

claim that both a lower landing speed and higher cruise speed could be obtained without any penalty in load-carrying ability. In a gesture that was typically courageous, Ballanca offered to forfeit payment if his wings did not live up to his claims. Unable to pass up such a tantalizing proposition, the Post Office Department drew up a contract for $7,000.

The deadline for completion was June 15, 1923, a date which Bellanca was unable to meet due to unforeseen difficulties. Having missed the official night-flying trials, he hoped to enter a Bellanca-de Havilland in the *Detroit News Air Mail Trophy* competition, the seventh event at the National Air Races in October 1923. Had the Air Mail Service agreed to the participation of the modified mail plane, G. M. Bellanca would have had two planes to watch at the races since, as has already been noted, the C.F. was among the entrants in the Aviation Country Club of Detroit event. Sixteen de Havillands, twelve of which finished the race, made up the Air Mail Trophy competition. Among the pilots were Bill Hopson and the legendary Jack Knight.

The race would certainly have been more interesting had the Bellanca-de Havilland not been barred from competition. With a top speed of 130 mph, it was 10 to 20 mph faster than other DH-4s. More importantly, whereas the standard de Havilland mail plane landed at 60 mph, G. M. Bellanca's version landed at a much more forgiving 40 mph, a decidedly safer situation in the event of an engine failure at night.

Mr. Bellanca's new wings, wrote the designer's friend and associate John Carisi late in 1924, *mounted on one of the standard de Havilland airplane bodies, outperformed to the astonishment of all who witnessed the test every one of the other new and purposely designed planes purchased at a much greater price than his wings.*[15]

Giuseppe Bellanca left Omaha to return to New York where, in the fall of 1923, he formed the Bellanca Aircraft Company. Victor Roos, his erstwhile partner, was equally unwilling to concede defeat in aviation and went on to business associations with Clyde Cessna, and with the Swallow, Lincoln, and Porterfield companies. In the Farmingdale, Long Island, factory once occupied by Lawrence Sperry, G. M. Bellanca rebuilt in 1924 three more de Havilland mail planes for the Air Mail Service. These were placed in service, along with the first, on the treacherous night routes between Cheyenne, Omaha, and Chicago, and were very popular.

The plane will excel the standard DH in the following points, stated Ernest M. Allison, one of the pilots assigned to fly the modified de Havillands, *load carrying, short landing, quick getaway, fast climbing and cruising speed. I like it better in every respect than the standard DH.*[16]

Bellanca ardently believed in the modification and wrote: *As for the quality of the wings, I honestly believe there are none in existence as efficient as they are. I believe that these wings, besides landing as slow as a Jenny and cruising and climbing faster than a standard DH, have a lifting capacity as high as two thousand pounds payload, more or less the same lifting capacity as the Martin bomber, with the advantage of making more speed . . . and using one Liberty motor instead of two.*[17]

The designer also pointed out in a letter that, where a normal DH-4 could not remain airborne, a Bellanca-winged mail plane could. *The pilots say that a common thing to happen to the Liberty motor is to have one carburetor out of commission and consequently six cylinders out of action. Yet, the remodeled DH plane in that condition would be able to get home.*[18]

Despite all this, additional orders from the Post Office Department did not materialize. In March 1925, an especially lean time in the already marginal business of being an aeronautical engineer, G. M. Bellanca sadly gave up the

Giuseppe Bellanca designed the WB-1 for the Wright Aeronautical Corporation of Paterson, New Jersey, which asked him to create a plane that would best demonstrate its new Whirlwind engine. With company employees on the wing, the Wright-Bellanca was photographed shortly before its first flight in September 1925. From left to right in front of the plane are Lieutenant Fred Becker, Charles Lawrance, Bellanca, and C. G. Peterson.

factory and allowed himself to be talked into joining the Wright Aeronautical Corporation of Paterson, New Jersey. His friend Clarence D. Chamberlin, who served as a test pilot for the company, had suggested to his employers that Bellanca was just the man to design a plane which would complement their very promising line of Whirlwind engines. Working from his design for the model C.G., Bellanca produced a six-seat cabin monoplane with five feet more wing span than the C.F., double lifting struts, and elegantly trousered wheels. Among the advanced features was the position of the pilot, who now sat ahead of the passengers in the enclosed cabin. It was christened the Wright-Bellanca WB-1.

Completed in the fall of 1925, the WB-1 was powered by a 200-hp J4 Whirlwind engine and followed the pattern set by its predecessor by surpassing even optimistic predictions of its performance. Top speed was 132 mph and cruise speed was 100 mph, while initial rate of climb was 900 feet per minute at a gross weight of 3,230 pounds. Flown by pilot Frederick H. Becker, it took first place for both efficiency and speed in event number five of the National Air Races at Mitchel Field, Long Island, being rated fifty-three percent more efficient than the nearest competitor. Also called the New York Air Races, this largest aviation meet in the country began on October 8, 1925, and lasted six days due to delays caused by high winds and bad weather. Among the endless lines of aircraft crowding the field were two old Bellanca C.E. airplanes, one of which crashed. Clarence Chamberlin, the owner and pilot,

44

Although bowlegged and ungainly, the Wright-Bellanca WB-1 proved to be a superb aircraft. Like the earlier C. F., it demonstrated unequalled efficiency in competitive air meets. Fred Becker, shown here at the controls, was hurt and the plane destroyed during an emergency landing early in 1926.

was injured while his passenger, Lawrence Burnelli, brother of aircraft designer Vincent Burnelli, was killed.

Chamberlin had modified the C.E. into a braced-wing monoplane but had not had the opportunity to probe its characteristics in the new configuration. He sustained a broken leg and ankle (though he was originally proclaimed dead in a mixup between passenger and pilot). His hospital stay of exactly a week—he refused to remain longer—cost $8.75, leaving him and his very understanding wife a grand total of $9.75 in the world. He was soon back in the air, however, cast and all.

The Wright-Bellanca WB-1 also participated at the National Air Races in the Merchants Association of New York Competition, in which it placed second to Casey Jones in his perennially successful clipped-wing Curtiss Oriole with its C-6 engine. Jones dominated the race from the very start, thrilling the crowd with an average speed around eight laps of 134.2 mph.

An attempt to set a world's unrefueled endurance record was conceived early in 1926, with thorough testing to be undertaken beforehand to determine the maximum load-carrying ability of the Wright-Bellanca. In the course of conducting speed and payload trials over a measured course at Mitchel Field, Fred Becker partially stalled the overloaded plane while turning in gusty conditions. The recovery demanded a landing at high speed at the neighboring Curtiss Field, but his excess momentum caused him to overrun the boundaries. He desperately hauled the plane back into the air to clear a rise separating Curtiss from the expanse of open ground that was Roosevelt Field, and the Wright-Bellanca suffered a landing-gear collapse. It somersaulted into a broken pile of wing panels, fuselage formers, splintered wood, and torn fabric.

Becker was badly injured but recovered to resume his flying career, a lucky escape for one of the U.S. Navy's first test pilots. The Wright-Bellanca was not so fortunate, but a second airplane was already under construction at the company facilities in Paterson, New Jersey. Designated the WB-2, it sported a more conventional landing gear, a steel-tube fuselage instead of wood, more cabin room, and other refinements. It was powered by the Wright J5 Whirlwind.

The J5 represented a major achievement in the design of aeronautical power planes, for it was the first truly reliable engine produced. While the J4 of the WB-1 had been quite good, it still had cooling problems which would probably not have allowed it to operate flawlessly for 33½ hours, a feat performed to the elation of the entire world by the J5 Whirlwind fitted to the *Spirit of St. Louis* during its Atlantic crossing. Reliable airplane structures had finally been built in World War I; the appearance of the Wright J5 in 1926 marked a comparable milestone in powerplants.

The Wright J5 Whirlwind engine was developed by S.D. Heron and Charles L. Lawrance, and produced 220 hp. In retrospect, its mating to the WB-2 is historic, as it was the first instance of virtually total reliability in an engine-and-airframe combination in one airplane. The globe-spanning records soon to be attained by so many men and machines were in great measure made possible by the Whirlwind, as well as the Wright Cyclone and Pratt & Whitney Wasp which soon followed; that so many of these records would be set in Bellanca monoplanes is a tribute to their designer.

The National Air Races for 1926 were held early in September in Philadelphia as part of the Sesqui-Centennial International Exposition. Flown by Lieutenant C. C. Champion, Jr., who achieved fame flying the Wright Apache biplane to amazing altitudes, the WB-2 easily won the efficiency trophy for the Aviation Country Club of Detroit event, although it placed fifth in speed behind a Pitcairn Sesqui-Wing, Casey Jones's clipped-wing Oriole, Walter Beech in his Travel Air 4000, and a Vought UO Corsair Navy fighter in civil guise. The Wright-Bellanca, wearing race number 140, also participated in a free-for-all speed competition in which it placed fourth.

The best single showing for the WB-2 came on the last day of the races. Entered in event number seventeen, the *Detroit News* Air Transportation Trophy competition, the monoplane swept the field in both speed and efficiency, a gratifying if not unprecedented victory for Giuseppe Bellanca. He had been heartbroken at the loss of the WB-1, which had been a bit faster but had lost the speed event the year before due to Fred Becker's lack of familiarity with the course. In the design of the WB-2, he had acceded to company demands that the aerodynamically clean "bent knee" landing gear be dropped and that the cabin be further enlarged. Even so, his latest plane had left the rest behind.

It was a less happy situation for the designer on the business front. Anxious not to alienate its customers, the Wright Aeronautical Corporation decided instead to give up its intended production of the spectacularly successful WB-2 and stick to making only engines. Bellanca considered offers from such companies as Huff-Daland in Pennsylvania, Ryan in California, and Beech in Kansas. In the end, he decided to accept a partnership with a New York millionaire named Charles A. Levine.

Just twenty-eight years old, Levine had made his fortune speculating in war-surplus munitions and equipment. His initially quite reasonable proposal

A major step in the development of aviation was the emergence of a truly reliable powerplant. The Wright J5 Whirlwind of 1926 was the first to deserve the title and made possible the transatlantic flight of Charles A. Lindbergh.

The Wright-Bellanca WB-2 had a steel-tube fuselage instead of the wooden structure of the WB-1, and was powered by the Wright J5 Whirlwind of 220 hp.

called for the formation of the Columbia Aircraft Corporation with G. M. Bellanca as president and a capital investment of $50,000. In deference to the designer, Wright Aeronautical passed up handsome offers—including one from a lanky pilot named Lindbergh who came with a certified check for $25,000 in hand—and sold the WB-2 and all production rights to Columbia. It was early 1927, and prospects for the future seemed all at once to be bright indeed.

With the plane came the special cabin fuel tanks built for an endurance flight which Wright had not undertaken after all. Clarence Chamberlin, who had conducted an extensive series of load and fuel consumption tests, agreed to stay on as the pilot of the WB-2 for the new company and proposed that they follow through with such a flight. Levine agreed and immediately brought in Lieutenant Leigh Wade, one of the celebrated Army aviators who had flown around the world in 1924, whom he felt would add to the publicity value of the venture. Personality differences surfaced in strong measure, a frequent occurrence around Levine, who was known to resort to his fists upon occasion, and Wade left. His replacement was the burly and colorful Bert Acosta.

Despite dire predictions that the plane would never leave the ground with 375 gallons of gas, Chamberlin and Acosta lifted the WB-2 off after only a fourth of the runway at Roosevelt Field had passed beneath their wheels, and climbed out with surprising ease. An anxious moment came early on when the fuel cutoff valve was accidentally hit, but the trouble was located and the engine restarted in time. The first night offered low clouds and gusting winds, but the weather improved and both men were able to sleep in shifts on a mattress and quilts thrown atop the fuel tanks. Thirst became the biggest problem when the water supply ran out, but determination drove the two pilots to husband the fuel supply carefully and remain aloft until the last drop of gasoline had been burned.

Their wheels touched ground at eighteen minutes to one on the afternoon of Thursday, April 14, 1927, two days after they had taken off. In remaining aloft for 51 hours 11 minutes 59 seconds, they had broken the world record established two years earlier by Maurice Drouhin and Jean Landry in France, who had themselves taken it from U.S. Army Lieutenants Oakley Kelly and John Macready. To the crowd of three thousand at the airfield and to the newspapers, however, it was an exciting event for a more important reason. The estimated ground track of 4,100 miles covered by Chamberlin and Acosta was 500 miles greater than the air distance to Paris.

Charles Levine had planned to produce an initial batch of ten WB-2s for the New York-to-Chicago airmail route, upon which he planned to bid. The tantalizing prospect of even more sensational headlines than those captured by the endurance flight prompted him to postpone such plans, however, and proclaim that the cabin monoplane would be groomed to fly the Atlantic. Since the name Wright-Bellanca was no longer appropriate, the WB-2 was formally rechristened the *Columbia* on April 24, 1927. On the same day, Chamberlin averted what might have been a serious accident by making an excellent one-wheel landing when a fitting broke on one main gear leg. His skill was especially appreciated since his passengers were Levine's eight-year-old daughter and a friend of hers.

Much of the suspense surrounding a New York-to-Paris flight was generated by a prize of $25,000 which had been posted by Raymond Orteig in 1919. It had lapsed after five years without a single attempt at the feat, at that time still beyond the ability of the airplane, but had been renewed for another five years in 1925. Bellanca and Chamberlin had talked of accomplishing such a flight the first year the Orteig Prize was offered, the designer assuring the pilot that he could build an airplane for the mission, but the prosperity of the late twenties was not yet at hand and work on that project never began.

It was with similar intentions that Charles A. Lindbergh, unsuccessful in his attempt to buy the WB-2 from Wright Aeronautical, later approached the Columbia Aircraft Corporation for the same reason. Levine accepted the offer of $25,000, but to the young pilot's dismay stated that a condition of the sale would be that a crew of the company's choice should make the flight. Since Levine had not applied in a proper and timely manner, the *Columbia* would be ineligible to win the Orteig Prize even if it were to be the first to fly between the named cities. Lindbergh had properly applied, and Levine saw his chance to grab the headlines he wanted while still making a profit on the sale of the plane. The airmail pilot, in return, would receive the Orteig Prize.

The proposition put forward by the millionaire was rejected due to his poor judgment of the twenty-five-year-old who sat across from him. Lindbergh was only interested in making the flight, a challenge he held as his dream. He wanted the Bellanca badly and had even cabled Giuseppe Bellanca repeatedly in December 1926, in the vain hope that another plane could be quickly constructed. The final obstacle he ran into, in the form of Charles Levine, drove him away to a struggling company in a broken-down building near the water in San Diego. It was only too happy to build for the clear-eyed visionary a single-engine monoplane also powered by the Wright J5 Whirlwind engine. The company was Ryan and the plane was the NYP (New York-to-Paris), soon to be christened the *Spirit of St. Louis*.

Selection of the crew for the Columbia monoplane, often referred to as the *Miss Columbia* in the press of the day, slowed the preparations for the proposed flight across the Atlantic. Levine wanted a more dashing and photogenic type than the boyish and moderate Chamberlin who, contrary to the contemporary image of the aerial daredevil, was a happily married teetotaler.

The designer of the plane intervened at this juncture, quietly but firmly bringing the weight of reason to the ticklish issue. "Mr. Bellanca's insistence," Chamberlin wrote later, "that I flew well even if I didn't film well, and knew his plane better than anyone else, was all that saved me."[19]

Bert Acosta was dropped from the crew, and Chamberlin and Lloyd Bertaud could not agree on key aspects of the flight, these recriminations resulting in the grounding of the *Columbia* by court order. Levine and Bertaud wanted a radio aboard, as the latter planned to follow the shipping lanes to Paris instead of the Great Circle route which both Lindbergh and Chamberlin knew to be the most direct. "I knew that we should be nearly 500 miles north of the ship lanes at the time when a radio could conceivably be of any value to us," Clarence Chamberlin remembered, "whereas the set had a range of only 125 to 150 miles."[20]

The excitement surrounding the New York flying fields grew toward a climax, its drama heightened by the danger inherent in seeking to cross the Atlantic by air. If anyone doubted that those planes were flying gasoline tanks, they had only to recall the fiery crash of the elephantine Sikorsky the year before from which the great French ace René Fonck was miraculously thrown clear. A further grim reminder came at the end of April 1927, when Noel Davis and Stanton Wooster were killed during a final load test at Langley Field, Virginia. Interest now centered on two aircraft, the trimotor Fokker *America* of Commander Richard E. Byrd, and the *Columbia*. The former had been damaged when it flipped on its back with Anthony Fokker himself at the controls at Teterboro, a field in northern New Jersey that had formerly been named Hasbrouck Heights.

An increasing flow of curious visitors came out to Curtiss and Roosevelt fields, all with an endless variety of questions. One elderly woman asked Clarence Chamberlin, whose sense of humor was always present in full measure, what would happen if a plane ran out of fuel while airborne.

"Ma'am," he replied with a straight face, "that is one of the tragedies of aviation. The good Lord only knows how many pilots are up there, out of gas and unable to get back to land!"[21]

Excitement reigned on the other side of the ocean, too. Another great French ace, Charles Nungesser, and a compatriot took off in a Levasseur biplane named the *L'Oiseau Blanc* in an attempt to fly the Atlantic from east to west. "DUE IN NEW YORK TOMORROW" proclaimed the headlines the following day. Sadly, Nungesser and Coli failed to arrive on the tenth. No trace of the gallant Frenchmen or their plane was ever found. Traversing the vast ocean in a fragile airplane was a risky venture indeed.

The arrival of Charles Augustus Lindbergh in the silver monoplane *Spirit of St. Louis* merited just the briefest of mentions in the back pages of the New York newspapers. The *Columbia* was the odds-on favorite to fly the Atlantic, having set the unrefueled endurance record weeks before, and few people paid any attention to the young pilot with the clear blue eyes. His Ryan NYP,

René Fonck, the famous French ace, poses in the cockpit of the mammoth Sikorsky S-35 trimotor biplane just before its first test flight late in August 1926. Fonck, who planned to fly the S-35 nonstop from New York to Paris, was miraculously thrown clear when it crashed on takeoff for Europe. The others aboard did not escape the flames.

Commander Richard E. Byrd, the famous explorer, planned to be the first to fly nonstop to Paris in the trimotor Fokker America. When it flipped on landing and was damaged, interest shifted to the Bellanca Columbia as the most likely to meet the challenge.

a plane built especially for the ocean crossing, was wheeled into a hangar at Curtiss Field, where Casey Jones took charge of last-minute preparations. It was a blind craft with big internal fuel tanks blocking all view forward. Lindbergh would have just a window in each door and a small periscope in the instrument panel.

Charles Lindbergh's quiet voice and serious responses to questions commanded attention, however, and he received increasing coverage from the reporters in attendance at the neighboring Curtiss and Roosevelt fields. He stated he would navigate by dead reckoning, he would go alone, he felt his plane had plenty of range, and, yes, he was confident he could stay awake. The flight was the important thing; the prize money would only allow him to reimburse the people back in Missouri who believed in him. There was no hesitation in "Slim" Lindbergh's manner as he paced off the runway at Roosevelt Field.

That rainy evening of May 19, wrote *New York Times* reporter Lauren D. Lyman, *there were lights in the hangar around the 'Spirit of St. Louis'; men were putting fuel in the big tank. A few doors away there were lights in the Bellanca hangar where Ed Mulligan of the Wright Company was making final adjustments to the Whirlwind engine. . . . Clouds were low and there was still a drizzle which was slacking off a bit.*[22]

It was a cold and wet spring morning when Lindbergh climbed into his overloaded plane. He opened the throttle wide and the *Spirit* gathered speed down the soggy runway, tires splashing as it bounced several times before taking off. Once over the telephone wires at the end of the field, the plane dipped to pick up flying speed and disappeared over the woods and gentle hills to the east. Left behind was the *Columbia,* fueled and ready but still grounded by the injunction which had been brought by Bert Acosta's lawyer.

This legal entanglement was resolved before the WB-2 took to the air on June 4, 1927. The plane was in peak condition, thanks to the careful ministrations of mechanic John Carisi, but a crowd lined the runway too closely and caused the first takeoff attempt to be aborted. Seated beside Chamberlin was Charles Levine, whose intention to make the flight had been carefully concealed since his wife had vowed to burn the plane before letting him attain the distinction of becoming the first airplane passenger across the Atlantic.

Since Lindbergh had reached Paris two weeks before, it was planned that the *Columbia* would press on all the way to Berlin. A solid cloud mass and fog down to the ground forced Chamberlin to circle before dawn on the second night, causing needed fuel to be burned off over the continent and disorienting the crew. When the tanks finally ran dry, Chamberlin set the rugged monoplane down in a wheat field near Eisleben. The Wright-Bellanca had been in the air forty-three hours, during which time its Whirlwind engine had never faltered.

Charles A. Lindbergh flew nonstop from New York to Paris in his Ryan NYP Spirit of St. Louis *on May 20–21, 1927. Lindbergh had initially tried to buy the Bellanca* Columbia *for his solo attempt.*

Bad weather before dawn and the resultant fuel depletion caused the Columbia *to land at Cottbus rather than Berlin. Chamberlin and Levine were unhurt in the resultant noseover. This flight was just one of a number of records set by the plane, also called* Miss Columbia, *and it became the most famous Bellanca.*

The WB-2 became famous as the Columbia *in which Clarence Chamberlin, shown here climbing out of the plane, and Charles Levine flew non-stop from New York to Germany in June 1927.*

An interesting note is that Chamberlin and Levine had spotted the U.S. Navy cruiser *Memphis* heading west in the North Atlantic from their airplane. Headed home on that ship to a hero's welcome and tickertape parade in New York City was Captain Charles A. Lindbergh.

The record-setting flight of the *Columbia* built upon that of the *Spirit of St. Louis*, adding one more element necessary to the realization of the dream of commercial transatlantic air travel. While the Ryan NYP was specially constructed for the rigors of the Atlantic flight, the Wright-Bellanca monoplane was a commercial type designed for production. The only special preparation made was the removal of the rear cockpit seats for the installation of additional fuel tanks. That it was capable of such phenomenal performance under these circumstances was indicative of the great strides being made in aviation during the latter half of the 1920s.

Charles Lindbergh selected the *Columbia* as his first choice for an Atlantic crossing precisely because it was the most efficient and technologically advanced airplane of its day. The Ryan was unquestionably a prettier aircraft, nevertheless, with its buffed metal cowling and silvery gray fabric over a sleek fuselage. Fate smiled when it allowed the tall, shy young man to realize his dream in the latter craft, for it was certainly the better suited to capture the imagination of the entire world and direct it skyward. Best of all, Lindbergh had done it alone in contrast to all other attempts, at once a dramatic and fittingly poetic pitting of man against the elements. Today the *Spirit of St. Louis* hangs in the National Air and Space Museum in the company of the Wright brothers' 1903 Flyer, two aircraft that have perhaps worked the greatest changes upon the course of history.

The Golden Age

Bellanca Pacemaker production began in 1928 with the CH-200, a six-passenger monoplane closely resembling the Columbia. *The forward location of the magnetos on the Wright J5 Whirlwind engine resulted in a bulged-nose appearance.*

Between the Atlantic flight of the *Spirit of St. Louis* and World War II, there was a flowering of aviation in the United States unparalleled in its diversity and scope. Great strides were being made with bewildering rapidity on all technological fronts in an evolution that ushered in NACA cowlings, retractable landing gears, wing flaps, deicer boots, radio range navigation aids, and the other elements necessary for the realization of safe commercial airline transportation. The all-metal Boeing 247 and Douglas DC-3 were a quantum leap forward from the wood-and-fabric Curtiss Condor biplane airliner of the late 1920s.

54

The Bellanca Pathfinder *nears comple-*
tion in the Bellanca Aircraft Com-
pany's temporary quarters at Port
Richmond, Staten Island, New York.
The special fuel tank for long-distance
flights is already in place in the cabin.

Giuseppe M. Bellanca stands in front
of a CH-300 Pacemaker in this photo-
graph probably taken late in 1929.

The Bellanca CH-300 offered excep-
tional performance and utility as a
seaplane. Rugged construction and the
ability to lift almost a ton of payload
made it a popular airplane in a
variety of roles.

54

The most visible element in this golden age of aviation was a profusion of thrilling record flights that filled the front pages of newspapers around the world in the late twenties and thirties. These flights, which made the name Bellanca a household word in all quarters, represented just the tip of the iceberg, although they did a great deal to change public perceptions and attitudes toward aviation. If a single-engine Bellanca could fly nonstop from New York to Istanbul, who could doubt that a twin-engine airliner could fly safely from Chicago to Cincinnati? Aviation was an open field for anyone with imagination, ability, and desire, and the siren call was often the drone of a Bellanca in flight.

Between Lindbergh's and Chamberlin's historic flights, Giuseppe M. Bellanca severed all connection with the Columbia Aircraft Corporation. Original plans had called for that company to construct WB-2 monoplanes for use on the New York-to-Chicago airmail route, upon which Charles Levine had bid. The Postmaster General refused Levine's petition, however, when it was discovered that he had entered into some contracts with the War Department that were being investigated by agents of the Department of Justice. This revelation hardly surprised the designer, who had already seen his hopes for the *Columbia* to be the first across the Atlantic dashed by his former associate's unethical dealings. Bellanca concluded, perhaps belatedly, that both aviation and his own interests would be better served if he looked elsewhere for financial backing.

This lesson in human nature was perhaps a necessary one for Giuseppe Bellanca, who, until shown otherwise, assumed all men shared his scrupulous honesty. His warm and loving nature, so well remembered by those who knew him, was always evident in his big smile, and complemented an innate dignity that bespoke his Mediterranean origins. Understanding his fellow man was at times more difficult than calculating stress loads or devising efficient airfoils.

The unfortunate association with Charles Levine was just another temporary setback to Bellanca, who was quickly back at work with forty employees under him in a plant at Staten Island. Several commercial CH monoplanes were built there, as well as the *Roma* and *Pathfinder* aircraft. In the fall of 1927, he accepted an invitation to move to Delaware, where the du Pont family, many of whom were pilots, had provided approximately $2,000,000 in capital. The Bellanca Aircraft Corporation initially occupied a facility with adjoining airfield on the Delaware River near Wilmington, before moving into a brand new plant at New Castle. Production of the CH resumed there, the Wright-powered versions being called Pacemakers and the more powerful Pratt & Whitney-powered monoplanes produced beginning in 1930, initially also termed Pacemakers, soon being called Skyrockets. These models were shortly to become famous for their remarkable achievements.

The rich legacy of the Bellanca C.F. continued. Its descendants were just as indisputably the most efficient airplanes of their day as the C.F. had been in 1922. Since only one example of the latter was built due to the economic conditions following World War I, an appreciation of the significance of the first Bellanca cabin monoplane may best be gained by studying those later Bellancas of similar line. Space limitations preclude more than the briefest mention of Bellanca aircraft models other than the CH series.

The Bellanca C.F. is today largely forgotten, but the glorious history of its progeny may very well reprieve it from a fate of ignominious obscurity. The globe-spanning achievements of these Pacemakers, Skyrockets, and special monoplanes are of such great magnitude that, even basking in reflected fame, the beautiful C.F. shines brightly. What follows is a brief chronological recounting of records set in Bellancas in what was truly aviation's golden age.

A Pacemaker flies over the Bellanca
Aircraft Corporation plant at New
Castle, Delaware. Below the plane is
an ample landing field located between
the factory and the Delaware River.

The Royal Canadian Air Force operated various Bellanca monoplanes.
These aircraft gained quick acceptance,
proving to be ideally suited to the
demands of bush flying in rugged
wilderness areas.

First of the Pratt & Whitney-powered Bellancas was the CH-300-W Pacemaker of 1930. Equipped with a 9-cylinder R-985 Wasp Junior air-cooled radial engine rated at 300 hp, this series featured a new rudder with a rounded top and greater area.

The interior of the CH-300 Pacemaker offered luxurious appointments and ample headroom. Large windows provided excellent visibility for the pilots and four passengers.

Less boxy than the later Bellancas, this early Pacemaker in military markings might almost be taken for a Fairchild 24 were it not for the lifting struts.

Below:
The Pacemaker also enjoyed success as an airliner, providing the last word in safety, comfort, and economy. Rapid Air Transport operated a route between Omaha and St. Louis in 1930.

The Shell Petroleum Company was one of a number of corporations to operate the Wasp-powered Bellanca CH-400 as a business airplane. (Rudy Arnold Collection/NASM)

Higher performance was the chief selling point of the Bellanca CH-400, the first production series to bear the name Skyrocket. The standard engine was the 420-hp Pratt & Whitney C-1 Wasp, although customers could also buy the plane with the 450-hp SC-1 Wasp. Factory selling price was $21,000.

Wheel pants and a speed-ring cowling further improved the performance of the Pacemaker in the Model E of 1932. This aircraft is one of three operated by the Airways Division of the Department of Commerce.

In contrast to its predecessors, the
Bellanca Senior Skyrocket of 1935 was
both larger and much more powerful,
although the basic design remained
little changed. This example is shown
in its natural element, participating in
an oil survey in Fort Nelson, British
Columbia, just prior to World War II.

By 1935, the Pacemaker had evolved
into a rugged workhorse that was as at
home hauling mining equipment in
remote parts of the world as it was
transporting passengers. This 1936 Senior Pacemaker, one of six built, had a
wingspan of 50 feet 6 inches, and a
gross weight of 5,600 pounds, with a
420-hp Wright R-975-E3 engine.

One of three Bellanca CH-400 Sky-rockets acquired by the U.S. Navy in 1932, the RE-3 was transferred to the Marines, who used it as a flying ambulance.

A party of skiers is transported to the mountain regions of Norway by a seven-place Bellanca Senior Pace-maker. The more powerful engine combined with a controllable pitch propeller and full NACA cowling, and the very capacious fuselage, endowed the Model 31-42 with greater utility than earlier Bellancas.

Below:
In 1937, the Navy purchased a Bellan-ca Model 31-55 Senior Skyrocket and designated it the JE-1. More powerful than its civilian counterparts, it was fitted with a 570-hp Pratt & Whitney R-1340 radial engine.

The *Columbia*, as already described, flew nonstop to Germany early in June 1927, and was brought back later in the summer. This most famous of Bellancas then made the first nonstop flight to Havana from New York in 1928, piloted by Wilmer Stulz, who that year also piloted the Fokker in which Amelia Earhart became the first woman to cross the Atlantic Ocean by airplane.

The year 1928 also saw two endurance records set in Bellancas. Army Lieutenant Royal V. Thomas established a new mark of 35 hours 25 minutes,

61

The Noorduyn Norseman of 1936 shows the influence of Giuseppe Bellanca and his monoplanes in its structure. Designed by Robert Noorduyn and built in Canada, it is reminiscent of Bellanca airplanes in its cockpit, tail, and landing gear. Noorduyn, well known for his association with his compatriot Anthony Fokker, worked for Bellanca from 1929 to 1932.

The size of the Senior Skyrocket belied the fact that it was fast, with a cruise speed of 160 mph, and light on the controls.

in the monoplane *Reliance*, in which he was subsequently killed. Edward Schlee and William S. Brock broke Chamberlin and Acosta's record of the year before with a new unrefueled endurance time of 59 hours 7 minutes, in the Bellanca *Rose Marie* over San Diego, California.

Bellanca chief test pilot George Haldeman started the year 1929 with a nonstop flight from Canada to Cuba in February. Martin Jensen set a new solo endurance record of 35 hours 33 minutes, in the *Green Flash*, and the teenage Elinor Smith established a similar record for women of 25 hours 23 minutes.

Another famous Bellanca, the Green Flash, *receives the attention of Bellanca and Wright Aeronautical specialists. Martin Jensen set a new solo endurance record in this plane of 35 hours 33 minutes in 1929, and Roger Q. Williams initiated a nonstop flight to Rome in it, although a takeoff accident put an end to the attempt.*

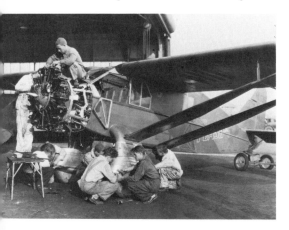

Roger Q. Williams and Lewis A. Yancey pose with Giuseppe M. Bellanca in front of a Pacemaker. In July 1929, Williams and Yancey flew nonstop from Old Orchard, Maine, to Santander, Spain, in the Bellanca Pathfinder.

Right:
Edward Schlee and William S. Brock broke the unrefueled endurance record set by Clarence Chamberlin and Bert Acosta in 1927, remaining airborne in the Bellanca Rose Marie *for 53 hours 7 minutes in October 1928. They are shown here in front of another Bellanca monoplane.*

Roger Q. Williams and Lewis A. Yancey flew nonstop from Old Orchard, Maine, to Santander, Spain, in July 1929. Williams had earlier tried to fly to Rome in the *Green Flash*, but an accident at takeoff had dispelled all hopes for using this plane in such a flight. Williams and Yancey had better luck with the *Pathfinder*, a Bellanca formerly christened the *North Star*, and were well satisfied with having reached Spain although the Italian capital was still their intended destination. On the home front, Bellanca won five firsts, three seconds, two thirds, and two fourths out of seven events they entered in the 1929 National Air Races. As was traditional, first place in both efficiency contests was taken by Bellanca aircraft.

George W. Haldeman established an altitude record for commercial air-

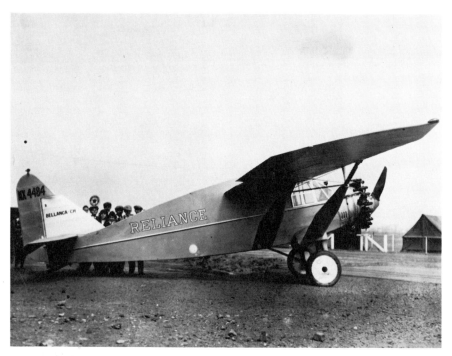

Briefly christened North Star *for a flight that never materialized, the Bellanca J NX-3789* Pathfinder *successfully flew from Maine to Spain. Although Williams and Yancey landed short of Rome, their intended destination, their achievement was nonetheless remarkable.*

Opposite:
Army Lieutenant Royal V. Thomas established a solo endurance record in a Bellanca CH-200 in 1928, remaining aloft 35 hours 25 minutes. He was later killed in a crash while attempting to establish another record.

Russell Boardman hoped to fly from Nova Scotia to Ireland in this Bellanca CH-300 in the fall of 1928. Although bad weather and damage to his plane prevented his attempt, he had far better luck the next year in the Cape Cod, *which he and John Polando flew to Istanbul.*

planes in a standard Pacemaker early in 1930, attaining the remarkable altitude of 30,453 feet. Elinor Smith claimed the altitude record for women in a similar endeavor in which she reached 27,418 feet. Both efficiency contests at the 1930 National Air Races were yet again won by Bellancas, and the third consecutive first place in the *Detroit News* efficiency event won for the Bellanca Aircraft Company permanent possession of the trophy.

A nonstop flight from New York to Bermuda and back brought the *Columbia* into the headlines again, the crew consisting of Roger Q. Williams, Captain J. Errol Boyd, and Navy Lieutenant Harry P. Connor. Later in the year, on October 10, 1930, the *Columbia* with Boyd and Connor aboard flew from Harbor Grace, Newfoundland, to the Scilly Isles, Great Britain. It was the third Atlantic crossing by a Bellanca and the second for the *Columbia.* Time en route was 23 hours 40 minutes.

The following year was one that further emblazoned the name of the Italian-born designer across front pages. The Packard-Bellanca, powered by the Packard DR-980 nine-cylinder diesel radial engine, established the amazing unrefueled endurance mark of 84 hours 33 minutes, on May 28, 1931, in Jacksonville, Florida. The fourth Atlantic flight by a Bellanca was that of the red-and-white *Liberty,* which was flown by Danish-born Holger Hoiriis with Otto Hillig as passenger and sponsor. Taking off on June 24, and encountering fog and rain squalls, the *Liberty* flew on by dead reckoning to find that northerly winds had brought it far south of course. As a result, this plane landed in Krefeld, Germany, the place of Hillig's birth, before pressing on to Copenhagen, the crew enjoying a hero's welcome in both countries.

While still in Harbor Grace, Newfoundland, Hioriis and Hillig had met Wiley Post and Harold Gatty, who were preparing to depart in the beautiful white Lockheed Vega *Winnie Mae.* In a spirit of shared adventure, the

Two Peruvian fliers, Lieutenant Carlos Legarra of the navy and Captain Carlos Martino de Pinillos of the army, pose beside their Bellanca at Bolling Field in Washington, D.C., before attempting a record flight home in late May 1929.

While still a teenager, Elinor Smith set an unrefueled endurance record for women of 25 hours 23 minutes in June 1929.

In May, Elinor Smith set an altitude record for women of 27,418 feet over Roosevelt Field on Long Island, New York. Here she is shown examining the barograph immediately after the flight.

Bellanca Company pilot George Haldeman established an official altitude record of 30,453 feet in a standard Pacemaker early in 1930.

Powered by a Packard DR-980 9-
cylinder Diesel radial engine, this
Bellanca remained aloft without aerial
refueling for 84 hours 33 minutes on
May 28, 1931, over Jacksonville, Florida. Although the flight highlighted the
fuel efficiency of the Diesel powerplant,
for which the Bellanca was a test bed,
these engines did not gain acceptance.

Holger Hoiriis and Otto Hillig flew to
Germany, then on to Denmark, in the
Bellanca Liberty in June 1931.

Clyde Pangborn and Hugh Herndon, Jr., made the first nonstop flight across the Pacific Ocean in the Bellanca Miss Veedol, *taking off from Samishiro Beach, 280 miles north of Tokyo, on October 3, 1931. The 300-pound landing gear was dropped to decrease weight and extend the range, and the bottom of the plane was reinforced to withstand a belly landing. When the fliers landed in Wenatchee, Washington, forty-one hours later, they had covered 4,558 miles without incident. This photograph shows* Miss Veedol *at Boeing Field in Seattle after a new landing gear had been fitted.*

One of the most remarkable distance flights was that of John Polando, left, and Russell Broadman in the Bellanca Cape Cod. *Thanks to precise navigation, they flew nonstop from New York to Istanbul, Turkey, covering 5,014 miles in 49 hours 19 minutes in July 1931.*

Cesare Sabelli flew to Ireland in this Bellanca named Leonardo da Vinci *in May 1934.*

Bellanca crew exchanged handshakes and wishes for good luck with Post and Gatty, and followed their 8½-day flight around the world with great interest.

Two Bellancas took off within eighteen minutes of one another from Floyd Bennet Field in Brooklyn, New York, Giuseppe Bellanca's first American home, on July 28, 1931. The black-and-yellow *Cape Cod*, a Pacemaker with a 300-hp Wright engine, was flown by Russell Boardman and John Polando, who crossed nonstop from New York to Istanbul, Turkey. With remarkably precise navigation, they landed after having covered 5,014 miles.

The second plane to take to the air that morning was the famous *Miss Veedol*, a red Bellanca CH-400 powered by a 425-hp Pratt & Whitney Wasp. Flown by Clyde Pangborn and Hugh Herndon, Jr., who were following on the heels of Post and Gatty in an around-the-world flight, the plane became the first to fly nonstop across the Pacific, flying from Japan, across 4,500 miles of ocean in 41 hours 13 minutes, to land at Wenatchee, Washington. The landing gear had been dropped to save weight and reduce drag, so that *Miss Veedol* bellied in dramatically on American soil. *Miss Veedol* had been the fifth Bellanca to fly the Atlantic, passing the *Cape Cod*, which became the sixth.

Parker D. Cramer, an American who twice before had tried to fly to Europe via Greenland and Iceland, took off with Canadian Oliver Paquette at the end of July 1931. Flying a Bellanca Pacemaker seaplane powered by a 225-hp Packard diesel engine, the two men successfully completed the first flight ever made over Greenland as part of a planned trip to Copenhagen, Denmark. The feat was a daring one; what few coastal charts were available were unreliable, and the vast expanse of the icecap, which reached heights of 9,000 feet, was virtually unknown. There would have been little hope of survival in the event of a crash landing.

In July 1933, Stephen Darius and Stanley Girenas took off on a nonstop flight from New York to Kovno, Lithuania. The eighth Atlantic flight, in those days still as much of an adventure as the first, was made by the dashing Italian-American Cesare Sabelli and George Pond. Sabelli, whose dream had long been to fly nonstop to Rome, had originally attempted the flight in the huge *Roma* in 1928, but had failed due to a faulty engine. Six years later, on May 15, 1934, he was luckier in a smaller Bellanca named *Leonardo da Vinci*, although a fuel tank problem forced an intermediate landing in Ireland. The ninth crossing was that of two courageous Polish brothers, Ben and Joe Adamowicz, who returned to Warsaw after many years in the *Warszawa*, the old Bellanca *Liberty* (which, in the intervening years, had been rechristened *Olympia* in anticipation of a flight to Greece that never materialized). Then, in 1934, Dr. Richard Light and Robert Wilson flew the Bellanca Skyrocket seaplane *Asulinak* in an around-the-world flight.

Captain Stephen Darius and Stanley T. Girenas made the seventh nonstop crossing of the Atlantic Ocean in the Bellanca CH-300 Lituanica, *only to crash fatally upon landing at Soldin, Germany, on July 15, 1933. The original destination of these two fliers, who took off from New York two days earlier, was Kovno, Lithuania.*

With a new name, this Bellanca carried brothers Ben and Joe Adamowicz to Poland in 1934. The Warszawa, *previously named* Olympia, *was in fact the* Liberty *which had made the fourth nonstop crossing of the Atlantic by air in 1931. As neither brother could fly, Holger Hoiriis went along as pilot.*

The successes listed above belie the perils of undertaking large-scale flights in the days before adequate instruments, procedures, navigational aids, and weather data were available. If there were successes in Bellancas, there were also sobering failures. Cramer and Paquette were lost at sea due to engine failure between Lerwick, Shetland Islands, and Copenhagen, on August 9, 1931; *Miss Veedol*, renamed *The American Nurse*, was lost at sea without a trace in 1932; a winter attempt to fly the Atlantic had brought death the year before to Major William MacLaren and Mrs. Beryl Hart in the Bellanca *Trade Wind*; two additional flights to Scandinavia ended in Bellancas being ditched,

The last known photograph of the Bellanca Trade Wind *shows it taking off from Hamilton Harbor, Bermuda, on January 15, 1931, on the second leg of its Atlantic crossing. Major William MacLaren and Mrs. Beryl Hart were lost at sea; no trace of the plane was ever found.*

68

A fatal crash put an end to the Hochi-
Hinomaru *before its Japanese crew
could attempt the first east-to-west
Pacific crossing.*

*General Francesco de Pinedo planned
to fly nonstop to Persia in his Bellanca*
Santa Lucia, *but was killed in a tragic
crash on takeoff.*

the former *Roma* sesquiplane off Newfoundland and Kurt Bjorkvall's Pace-maker off the coast of Ireland. Darius and Girenas were killed in a crash during their attempt to reach Lithuania. Perhaps the worst disaster was the fiery crash on takeoff of the fuel-laden Bellanca *Santa Lucia*, in which the famous Italian aviator Francesco de Pinedo perished. While nobody claimed that crossing the oceans by air was safe, it was nevertheless universally maintained that one had the best chance of succeeding in a Bellanca.

*Cesare Sabelli, Roger Q. Williams, and
Captain Pietro Bonelli had to abort
their planned flight to Italy in the
Bellanca K* Roma, *a large sesquiplane
built in 1928 which featured a retractable landing gear and was powered by
a 500-hp Pratt & Whitney Hornet
engine. Renamed the* Enna Jettick *for
a flight to Norway by Thor Solberg and
Carl Petersen, it was ditched off the
coast of Newfoundland in 1932.*

The Bellanca TES, built for the Chicago Daily News *and christened* The Blue Streak, *was a push-pull aircraft powered by back-to-back 400-hp Pratt & Whitney engines. Excessive vibration in the extended propeller shaft resulted in a fatal crash.*

We are making airplanes today, Giuseppe Bellanca wrote late in 1928, *not for dramatic adventure, but to meet the swiftly rising demand for dependable means of air transport. . . . From my earliest experiments, twenty-two years ago, I have not deviated from my original objective, which was to design and build an airplane to unite the maximum safety and the greatest possible efficiency, as measured by speed, load, and range.*[23]

It is interesting to note that aviation in the United States benefitted greatly from foreign design engineers, many of whom settled in America. There were Igor Sikorsky and Alexander Kartveli from Russia, Jean Roché from France, and the Dutchman Anthony Fokker. Giuseppe Mario Bellanca, who died in 1960, was unquestionably a genius whose remarkable designs changed the face of aviation. Although his most famous plane, the *Columbia,* was destroyed in a hangar fire in 1934 which prevented it from becoming part of the Smithsonian Institution's National Aeronautical Collection, the very significant Bellanca C.F. will remain in a place of honor in the National Air and Space Museum. There it will be preserved for future generations to see, a tangible reminder of days and machines past.

The Bellanca P-200-A Airbus offered excellent utility as a cargo plane or a fifteen-passenger airliner. The depressed economic climate of the early 1930s, however, limited the market for such a plane. The improved Aircruiser version was very popular in Canada, where its load-lifting capabilities were lengendary.

Designed as a trimotor racer, this Bellanca Model 28-92 was christened Alba Julia 1918 in preparation for a projected nonstop flight to Budapest, Hungary.

Irish Swoop was a racer designed and built by Bellanca for participation in the 1934 MacRobertson Race. Although disqualified, it went on to cross the Atlantic in 1936 with Englishman James Mollison at the controls in the record time of just 13 hours 17 minutes. Bought by the Spanish Republicans, the plane was destroyed in the Spanish Civil War.

Fourteen Bellanca Airbuses, designated C-27s, were operated by the U.S. Army Air Corps in the mid-1930s.

Built for Colombia in 1934, the Bellanca Model 77-140 was a twin-engine development of the Airbus.

The Bellanca 14-9 Junior, which appeared in 1939, was the first in a line of general aviation aircraft which enjoyed a long production life after World War II.

Subsequent History of the Bellanca C.F.

The Bellanca C.F. and all production rights to its design were acquired in 1924 by the Yellow Aircab Company, an organization formed with the intention of providing aerial taxicab service. The carriage-type facing seats, with room for four and baggage, and the great economy of the cabin monoplane together with its gentle landing speed, all promised to make the Bellanca the ideal aircraft for such an undertaking (if there were, indeed, any market for such a service).

A number of structural modifications were carried out on the C.F. in its conversion to a Yellow Aircab. The entire front end of the fuselage, from the cabin forward, was chopped off and a new steel-tube engine mount was attached. Over this went a new sheet-metal cowling. The original wood landing gear was replaced with a steel unit, additional windows were placed at the cabin front, and the pilot's cockpit cutout was enlarged.

That the Yellow Aircab Company did not succeed is hardly surprising, for little if any demand for aerial taxis existed in 1925. The plane was next sold to the Continental Aircraft Corporation, a small company about which little is known. It, too, did not survive, and the modified C.F. was bought at auction by P. Gilberti of Hempstead, Long Island, on August 30, 1928. On December 10, 1928, he in turn resold it for $150, less engine and instruments, to a young man named William Stanly Smith.

"Smitty," as he was called around Roosevelt Field, was a would-be pilot who set about restoring the C.F., which he planned to use for exhibition purposes. The plane was fitted at this time with a 110-hp Anzani radial engine, a slightly more powerful version of the unit that had first powered it. The original propeller was reworked by the Cessna Company. On December 11, 1930, Smitty applied to the Aeronautics Branch of the Department of Commerce for a registration number and was given 11036, which he painted on the rudder. Records show the plane at this point to have been fitted with a 35-gallon fuel tank. When the student pilot next contacted the Department of Commerce, it was to obtain permission to have the C.F. flown from Roosevelt Field to Glenn H. Curtiss Airport, which had been relocated in North Beach, Long Island. For this purpose, it was licensed in the restricted category and became NR-11036 for its first cross-country flight in many years, which was successfully carried out on October 4, 1931. By this time, the plane had apparently been modified to take a 50-gallon fuel tank. This larger tank left no room for a firewall, so that only a few inches of open space separated the engine accessory case from the tank, hardly the best of arrangements in the event of a crash. Another departure from Giuseppe Bellanca's original design was a modification which added a vertical stabilizer where formerly there had been just a rudder, but just when this change was made is not known.

One of those who helped Smith fix the Bellanca was veteran pilot Paul Kotze, who also gave the young student pilot flying lessons from time to time. When the day of the test flight for the renovated monoplane arrived, it fell to Kotze to be the pilot. It was a very bad day, however, with a high wind and 200-foot ceiling, and as the restoration crew stood looking at the sky, Bert Acosta

In 1924, the Bellanca C.F. was sold to the Yellow Aircab Company, which planned to operate a fleet of the monoplanes as aerial taxicabs. Although the seating capacity and economy of the "Yellow Aircab," as the C.F. was renamed, made it ideal for such employment, no market was found, and no additional aircraft were built. (Courtesy U.S. Air Force)

Among the modifications performed to convert the C.F. into a "Yellow Aircab" was the substitution of a steel-tube landing gear for the original wooden unit. (Courtesy U.S. Air Force)

approached. Kotze, who is still active in Long Island aviation at the Cradle of Aviation Museum, recalls that Acosta asked what they were doing. Upon hearing that the Bellanca was to be tested, he proclaimed it to be one plane he had never flown and insisted upon taking it up.

He took off crosswind, Kotze remembers, and made a chandelle turn right up into the clouds and around, and flew up above the layer of clouds for about fifteen or twenty minutes. Then he came down below, landed it, and apologized for forcing us to let him fly the aircraft.

Paul Kotze himself became well acquainted with the C.F. shortly thereafter, and his impressions of flying it are still sharp. *You have no forward*

The modified Bellanca C.F. sits in the foreground of an aircraft display held on September 20, 1931, at the Glenn H. Curtiss Airport on Long Island. Also being shown to the public are a Curtiss Model D Headless Pusher, a Thomas-Morse S-4C Scout, and the giant twelve-engine Dornier Do X flying boat. (Courtesy Gordon Swanborough)

This poor-quality photograph of the C.F. shows it on display at the old Roosevelt Field Air Museum around 1932. Note that the vertical tail has been changed to include a stabilizer. The civil registration number 11036 can just be made out on the rudder. (Courtesy Lewis R. Berlepsch)

visibility whatsoever, he stated emphatically. *I taxied around and wondered how the hell Bert flew his plane. Then I realized that from the cockpit you can look down into the cabin area, and through the side windows you can see the runway nicely. So I decided that I was going to fly it and away I went, watching the runway through the windows. It was going along well, I got in the air, and gee, it flew beautifully! So, at the end of the flight, I felt I had to duplicate that by coming in for a fine landing. I stuck my head in the cockpit again and looked through those windows, and it came down beautifully. Nothing to it. I liked that airplane!*[24]

Sadly, William S. Smith was not able to enjoy the fruits of his efforts, as he was killed propping another airplane on October 25, 1931. At this point, the C.F. became part of the old Roosevelt Field Air Museum, sharing quarters with a Curtiss D Headless Pusher, the Thomas-Morse S-4C Scout belonging to Kotze, and many other famous aircraft. These aircraft were flown upon occasion, the C.F. by both Kotze and Sonny Harris.

With the passing years, the Roosevelt Field museum disintegrated, and the C.F. was transported to the Bellanca home in Galena, Maryland, a beautiful estate with its own airfield located a few miles up the Sassafras River from the Chesapeake Bay. There it sat for many years until its existence was brought to the attention of the National Air Museum in Washington, D.C. On July 21, 1961, less than a year after the death of Giuseppe Mario Bellanca, it was officially donated and trucked to the museum's facility in Silver Hill, Maryland.

Even as it now stands, then Head Curator Paul E. Garber wrote to Mrs. Dorothy Bellanca, referring to the condition of the plane, *this airplane is a wonderful example of the genius of your distinguished husband, and we will be proud to maintain it as a memorial to his eminent place in aeronautical history.*[25]

It was to be almost twenty years before museum exhibit requirements and the relative needs of more than two hundred other aircraft would allow the Bellanca to be restored. At that time, it was almost sixty years old.

Restoration

Karl Heinzel and Richard Horigan were the craftsmen assigned to restore the C.F. Here they examine photographs of the plane taken in 1922. Since little in the way of original drawings and documentation was available, the restoration team had to rely heavily upon photographic evidence.

The Bellanca C.F. was brought into the restoration shop at the Paul E. Garber Preservation, Restoration, and Storage Facility in Silver Hill, Maryland, on January 25, 1979. After almost twenty years of storage, its turn had at last come to receive the painstaking attention of the highly skilled craftsmen of the National Air and Space Museum.

Renamed in 1980 in honor of Historian Emeritus Paul Edward Garber in appreciation of sixty years of dedicated service, during which he saved many unique aircraft from destruction, this facility is today a museum in its own right. Visitors on regular tours see more than a hundred airplanes in five buildings, with additional display areas to be opened in the near future.

The highpoint of every tour is Building 10. In its three large bays, fourteen specialists work to make four aircraft new again each year. It was into this clean and well-lighted center of activity that the C.F. was brought, forlorn and bereft, to find itself in the company of a single-seat Northrop flying wing, a Vought F4U-1D Corsair, the Langley Aerodrome A of 1903, and the only remaining Nakajima J1N1-S, a Japanese night-fighter nicknamed *Irving* by the Allies during World War II.

Richard D. Horigan, Jr., and Karl Heinzel were the craftsmen assigned the restoration. They began with a preliminary inspection of the Bellanca monoplane, noting various details of the work awaiting them. The passing years had not been kind to the airplane, and a further complication was the fact that it had been substantially modified. The fabric, long gone from the wings and fuselage, had allowed parts to break away and become lost, and had contributed to the degree of corrosion evident on all metal fittings. To further complicate the restoration process, the horizontal stabilizer, elevator, and rudder were missing altogether and would have to be made from scratch. Cracking, shrinkage, and other signs of general deterioration showed in the wood surrounding the enclosed cabin, although it was hoped that the original varnish might have prevented the faded red paint on its surface from actually penetrating the grain.

The earlier landing gear would have to be reconstructed, too, since it had long ago been replaced with the steel type found on the plane. This meant that suitable wheels and tires would have to be located as well, often a very difficult proposition in restoring a plane as old as the Bellanca C.F. The exhaust collector ring would not be retained since the C.F. had originally featured curved individual stacks. These would be reproduced to match existing photographs. The rear fuselage structure, which had broken off and needed repair, and an entirely new tail skid would have to be built as the original one was missing entirely. This list grew longer as Karl and Rich examined each section of the C.F. It would not be one of the most difficult restorations either technician had tackled, but it would nevertheless demand a great deal of time and attention.

Any such project also requires curatorial work, accomplished by curators in the main museum building eight miles away. Curator of Aircraft Robert C. Mikesh combined research materials with working guidelines, a task he

This is how the C.F. looked at the start of restoration in January 1979. Immediately evident to museum personnel were the incorrect cowling and landing gear, broken rear fuselage, and general deterioration of the wood, which had been painted red around the enclosed cabin.

Rich Horigan carefully uses a wooden block and hammer to loosen the plywood covering the sides of the C.F. cabin. The old wood was too far deteriorated to be salvaged, although most of the internal structure was found to be in good condition.

undertakes for every airplane restored by the National Air and Space Museum. In the course of these preparations, the Bellanca family was contacted to see what might be available in the way of original drawings and photographs. Help was provided throughout the project by August T. Bellanca, himself an aeronautical engineer and president of the Bellanca Aircraft Engineering Company. Many of his famous father's papers had been kept over the years, so that he was able to provide some construction sketches and photographs.

It was hoped at the outset that the original wooden sides of the C.F. might be salvaged, but that proved to be impossible when a more thorough examination revealed them to be unworthy of retention. In addition to excessive deterioration, some of the wood at the front had been cut away when the Yellow Aircab Company added extra windows. New wood could not be added without making an obvious seam. The door was in good enough condition, however, to allow it to be restored and used again, so that at least this small section of the original skin from 1922 would be retained.

Regardless of the care taken to match original materials and techniques, a bit of authenticity is lost with each replacement. It is part of the function of the National Air and Space Museum to preserve its unique collection for future generations, and the retention of deteriorating materials would not fulfill this obligation if they would then endanger the restored airplane. All factors must be weighed to ensure that the best compromise has been reached between preservation and replacement.

Aviation plywood comes in the standard size of four feet by eight feet. For this restoration, oversize sheets of plywood were required. What might have been an extremely difficult problem was quickly solved by the Aero Supply Company of Harrisonville, Missouri, which generously produced a special run of mahogany plywood in sheets measuring five feet by eleven feet.

The underlying wooden structure of the fuselage appeared to be in reasonably sound condition, needing a thorough cleaning to remove old varnish as well as general repair. Chemical treatment removed corrosion from metal fittings and cables taken out of the plane. These parts were then further treated to ensure their continued freedom from rust. Once this had been accomplished, they were set aside until needed for reinstallation.

Karl Heinzel, who had previously participated in the restoration of the Lockheed XP-80, took on the task of building up a completely new landing gear. Working from photographs and rough plans, he first reproduced the metal fittings. Then the airplane was leveled, and he began constructing the gear legs and spreader bar out of ash, basswood, and balsa, in place under the C.F.

The plans I had to work with were enough to give me the rough dimensions like the length and the width, he stated, *but the actual alignment could not be accomplished on a table, as some of the parts sit off at a slight angle to one another. I had to hold the entire assembly together with clamps to get all the little angles to fit just right before I could glue the mahogany side pieces on, that hold the whole thing together.*[26]

It appeared from photographs that Jenny wheels and tires had been used on the C.F. This was logical since Curtiss JN-4 parts were widely used in 1922, and the gross weight of both planes matched quite closely. While these wheels were on hand, an extra set of original tires was not. Luckily, however, antique automobile tires were found to match in every dimension, and were treadless, as were the aircraft tires of the period in which the C.F. was built. These wheels and tires were incorporated into the restoration, and there remained only the wheel covers Karl had made up to complete the landing-gear assembly. How to attach the cloth covers was initially a mystery, since early photographs clearly showed the absence of any screw heads or other means of attachment. The first American-built de Havilland DH-4 bomber was brought into the restoration shop at this time, though, and Karl was delighted to note that it had the same type wheel covers. The technique was duplicated and this part of the restoration was finished.

Removing the cowling revealed that the original wooden engine mount had been replaced at some point with a steel-tube assembly. Between the fuel tank and the 110-hp Anzani engine are the accessories. The firewall was apparently deleted when a larger fuel tank was fitted around 1931.

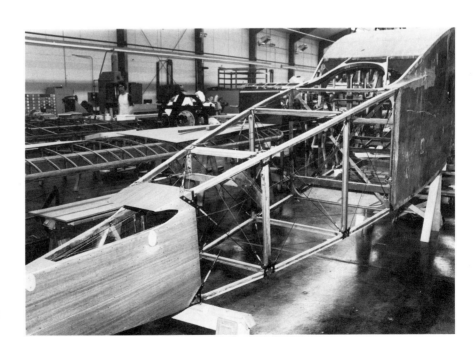

Working from back to front, Rich Horigan brought the fuselage back to virtually new condition. Note that the damage to the tail box has been completely repaired. In the background are the wings of the C.F.

Entirely new tail surfaces had to be built from scratch. Altogether, the rudder, elevators, and horizontal stabilizer took Rich Horigan a month to construct.

Rich Horigan holds the new rudder built for the C.F.

It is interesting to speculate whether or not the C.F., which was built at the airmail hub of Omaha, might have been influenced originally by the presence of converted de Havilland DH-4 mailplanes. The technique for affixing the wheel covers used on these aircraft, which were present in substantial numbers at the time the Bellanca first flew, could very easily have been copied by Giuseppe M. Bellanca and his crew. If so, it is ironic that history repeated itself almost sixty years later.

While Karl worked on the undercarriage, Rich Horigan was completing the fuselage. The side panels were put on first, then the top and bottom panels. These sheets of plywood had been cut to a shape slightly larger than was necessary to allow for last-minute corrections in positioning before they were nailed and screwed into place, and the excess wood was trimmed. The screw heads were all aligned to the direction of flight since this is how they had been found before restoration work began. Difficulties arose at the upper front of the side panels, which curve in above the engine cowling, and along the side of the open cockpit for the pilot, behind the wing, where there is a compound curve.

Combining sketches with photographic evidence, full-size drawings were prepared for the horizontal stabilizer, elevator, and rudder. These parts took Rich about ten days each to reproduce, after which he built a new tail skid. The latter was made of ash with a metal pivot point and shoe. These parts were installed in the repaired rear fuselage, although the control surfaces would have to come off again when the time came to apply their fabric covering.

The interior of the aircraft presented a major challenge since there was no photographic evidence of the original appointments and other details. While the C.F. had initially had a 35-gallon fuel tank according to fragmentary records, the restorers found that there was now a 50-gallon unit in it. The smaller tank had allowed two different seating arrangements, with all passengers facing forward or those in the front seat facing the rear seat, but the 50-gallon tank permits only the club seating arrangement. As there are no drawings of the smaller tank installation, it was decided to retain the bigger one since it was part of the plane's history and would be more original than any guesses Rich or Karl could make in fabricating and installing a smaller tank.

The cockpit area also presented mysteries. Throttle and carburetor heat linkages and cables were missing, as was the throttle itself. The cumulative experience of museum craftsmen is often called upon to fill in missing details, but the decision was made this time not to reproduce these items as even an educated guess could possibly lead future researchers astray in their study of past technology. It is unfortunate that only one Bellanca Model C.F. was built, since there is little chance that photographs or drawings will turn up to illustrate the original installation, although museum curators never give up hope of a lucky find.

Rich Horigan is an excellent woodworker and experienced craftsman, a fact attested to by the Albatros D Va fighter of World War I that had been his last project, one chronicled in an earlier entry in the Famous Aircraft of the National Air and Space Museum series. Under Rich's careful ministrations, the instrument panel, pilot's seat, and seatbelt were repaired and reinstalled, the belt requiring new leather since the original one had long ago rotted away. Rich also built from scratch a new walking beam. This metal unit translates fore-and-aft motion on the control stick, relayed further back into the fuselage by a rod near the base of the stick, into up-and-down motion through cables to the elevator.

While Rich concentrated on the fuselage, Karl was hard at work on the

The spartan instrument panel is mounted against the back of the rear passenger seat and the right side of the fuselage. Clockwise from the top left are the oil pressure and oil temperature gauges, the magneto switch, and the tachometer.

wings and lifting struts, which were in decidedly poor shape, in part because the original casein glue had lost its hold. Many ribs were flattened or broken, and a few were missing altogether. Shrinkage was a problem, and there were many cracks in both the ribs and the spars to attend to. Working outdoors in fresh air, Karl used acetone and a special paint remover to take away the chipped and cracked varnish, a dirty job which resulted in a great improvement in the appearance of these components. Indoors again, repair work began in earnest. Deformed ribs were brought back to shape and reinforced, and new wood was used to reproduce the original contours where shrinkage had taken place. Karl spliced in new wood only where it was absolutely necessary, however.

With its new tail surfaces attached, the Bellanca C.F. begins to look more like an airplane.

New aviation-quality mahogany-plywood skin encloses the cabin as the restoration progresses.

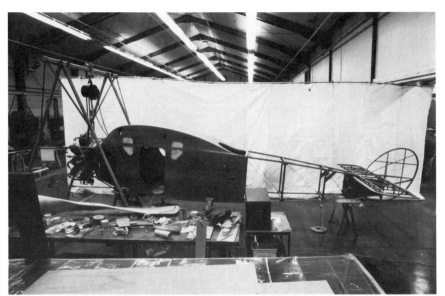

A closeup view of the rear fuselage shows the new appearance of the internal structure.

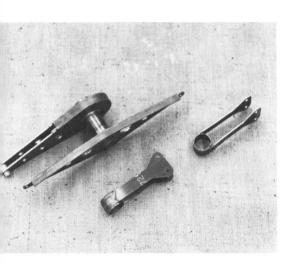

As many parts were missing, museum craftsmen had to produce these from scratch. Here is a walking beam, a part which translates fore-and-aft movement on the stick into up-and-down motion of the elevators.

Many long months after work began, Rich Horigan puts the finishing touches on the fuselage. The new plywood covering has now been completed, and careful attention has been given to following original screw and nail patterns. Here Horigan reinstalls the lift-strut fittings on the fuselage, which has been turned on its side to facilitate work.

Working outside in the fresh air, Karl Heinzel uses acetone and a paint remover to strip the old varnish from the wings.

Left:
Many ribs had broken noses, a common occurrence on very old aircraft. Although original wood was retained wherever possible, new wood was incorporated where necessary to build back the original contours.

The airfoil cross-section of the lift strut is evident in this view. To save weight, the spars were routed and the leading edge was built up of balsa wood.

Cleaned and treated control-cable pulleys are evident in this closeup view of one wing at the point where the aileron joins it. The aileron control horn had to be built up from scratch.

A very interesting feature of the C.F. was the use of ¼-inch cables attached to the wing spars which run down through the lifting struts to carry flight loads through the bottom of the fuselage. These cables allow the wing to be lighter in construction than would otherwise have been possible. The lifting struts themselves are true airfoils and contribute to the overall lift of the monoplane as well as increasing stability due to their great dihedral. A large amount of balsa wood was used in wing fillets, the strut leading edges, and the landing-gear spreader bar to reduce weight.

When originally built, the C.F. had straight wing tips. At some point in its career, these were rounded, although it is not known who performed this modification. Only general measurements and photographic evidence were available to assist in an attempt to change these tips back to the original configuration, so it was decided to allow this departure from the initial configuration of the C.F. to remain. The feeling was that keeping the wing-tip form with which the plane last flew was a more desirable alternative than making the guesses and arbitrary decisions inherent in returning to the squared tips. Therefore, replacement bows were made for each tip using the rotted bows as a pattern. The shaped wood around these tip bows was retained. For the same reason, the arrangement of the open cockpit was duplicated, although it is somewhat larger than the cockpit with which the C.F. first flew.

When the wing panels and struts were finished and revarnished, they looked virtually brand new. Karl put these aside and turned his attention to the propeller, which was apparently not the original unit, although it had the distinctive Bellanca shape and matched exactly the propeller seen in photographs from 1922. Karl found markings that indicated this prop had been

82

Curved exhaust stacks are fitted to the fully overhauled and preserved Anzani engine. These stacks were built of curved tubing which was specially manufactured outside the museum; bases were welded onto them so that they could be bolted to the exhaust ports.

manufactured by the Hartzell Propeller Company, and others to indicate that it had been reworked by the Sensenich Company for the Cessna Company. The involvement of Cessna was apparently accounted for by the fact that this company overhauled the Anzani engine fitted to the C.F. around 1930.

The propeller itself was in very good condition, requiring nothing more than a quick sanding and refinishing. The fabric tip was recovered and doped, a glossy olive color being applied to match its original paint.

In the meantime, Rich began tearing down the 110-hp Anzani engine. To ensure the longevity of restored airplanes, all components, including the engine, are taken down to the smallest parts and specially treated to inhibit corrosion. A cosmetic restoration would be much simpler and the end result would look every bit as good, but the interests of future generations would not be served by such superficial efforts. Steel tubing can rust from the inside out, dissimilar metals in contact with one another, if not treated, will corrode, exposed wood is subject to various kinds of decay, and so on. Work is planned and carried out at the Garber Facility with the understanding that each aircraft is to be carefully preserved as part of the aviation heritage of people the world over.

The Anzani, very similar to the engine that first powered the C.F., was complete and in good condition. Rated at 110 hp, it was overhauled and reassembled, the latter process taking longer than had been anticipated when it was discovered each rocker arm was a slightly different length. The engine could be made to run again, although the special preservatives which coat all internal surfaces and fill fuel and oil lines would have to be removed.

Individual curved exhaust stacks for the engine were made up from tubing that was commercially bent to the desired radius. The bases for these stacks were made up from scratch by Rich Horigan and Karl Heinzel both, and welded to the tubing. These were then bolted to the exhaust ports of the Anzani. Contrary to what one might expect, the bases have no holes, so that

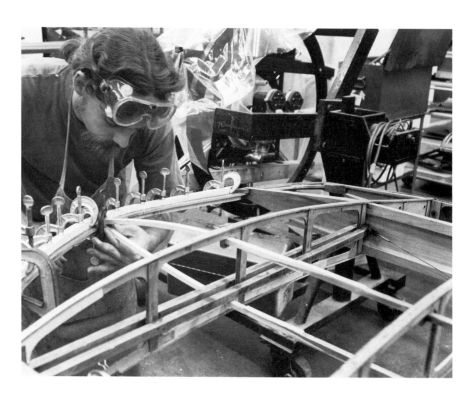

Karl Heinzel clamps a new bow in place on the right wing tip. Although the C.F. first flew with squarer tips, it was decided to keep the more rounded wing form since no original drawings were available to assist in an exact reconstruction.

83

Bill Stevenson skillfully builds up the cowling he has created for the restoration of the C.F.

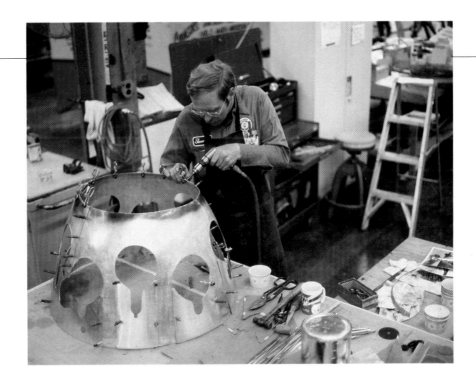

The first Bellanca cabin monoplane is shown completely disassembled, its wing panels in the foreground.

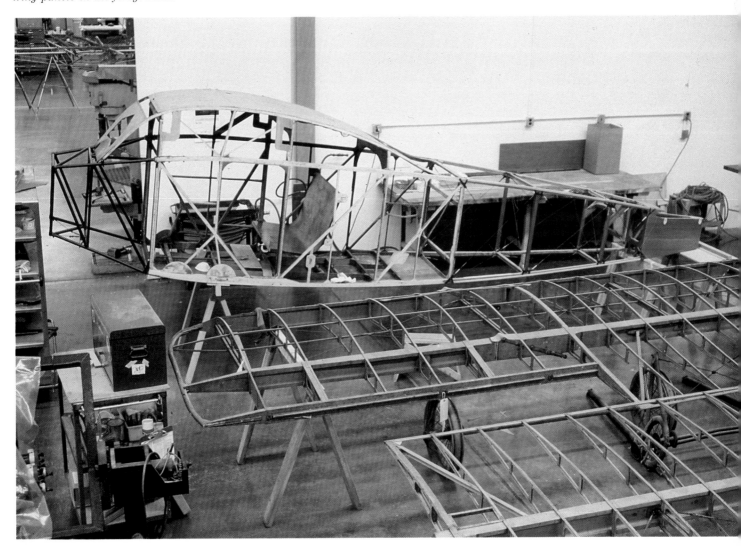

84

The C.F. nears completion in Building 10 at the Paul E. Garber Facility in Silver Hill, Maryland.

Just completed, the Bellanca C.F. is rolled out into the spring sunshine on May 13, 1980. Although not a difficult restoration, sixteen months and almost four thousand man-hours were required to bring the historic airplane back to virtually new condition.

Bill Stevenson, Rich Horigan, and Karl Heinzel stand in front of the plane they restored. For each, there is the special satisfaction of knowing he had a hand in this and other challenging projects.

Another view of the restored Bellanca C.F. shows its graceful lines and fragile elegance. The most efficient aircraft of its day, it was also one of the prettiest.

Metalsmith Bill Stevenson joined the restoration team to reproduce the original cowling of the C.F. He had performed a similar service for the restoration of the National Air and Space Museum's Albatros D Va of World War I.

Bill Stevenson put a great deal of effort into obtaining a perfect fit. Here he marks a cardboard pattern with a pen as an aid to reproducing a section of the cowling around one cylinder head.

Prior to fabric covering, the installation of a cowling, and other requirements in the restoration process, the C.F. was assembled and checked for alignment of parts. In this skeletal form, the plane attracted a great deal of interest from visitors.

they actually block off the exhaust outlets. This was done to prevent moisture or dust from entering the engine.

Bill Stevenson, another veteran of the Albatros D Va restoration, is a metalsmith whose skills are held in high esteem by his fellow craftsmen. The demanding task of re-creating the original cowling from photographs was given to him.

The most complex part of the cowling project was the area around the engine itself, Stevenson observed. *To cowl that properly took a tremendous amount of work with cardboard patterns. I went as closely as possible to the pictures of the aircraft, trying to keep in mind the ways they would have done it back then. The most fascinating thing to me was that they attached the cowling directly to the wood engine mount with wood screws. The engine is rigidly mounted so there was no need for much spacing around the cylinders to allow for torque.*

The Bellanca C.F. was assembled and checked for rigging before fabric was applied. Giuseppe Bellanca had designed the wing panels to come off and be reattached in perfect alignment in just a matter of minutes, an advanced feature the restoration team found especially handy. Visitors taking part in the regular tours of the Garber Facility found the skeletal monoplane a fascinating sight.

Close examination of the plane revealed hundreds of stamps made on the wood. These say "Duplicate Part by NASM" or "Repaired Part by NASM," and have the date the restoration work was performed. In order to avoid misleading researchers and historians in the future, it is the policy of the National Air and Space Museum to mark all replacements, as well as repairs, which might otherwise be assumed to have been made before the aircraft joined the museum collection.

Grade A cotton fabric was used to cover the fuselage, wings, lifting struts, and tail surfaces. The fuselage was covered with 36-inch fabric panels tacked in place in the manner that had originally been used. A small amount of apparently original fabric found near one aileron illustrated the manner in which wing fabric had been stitched, a technique the restorers copied. The early fabric also showed that very little dope had been used, apparently in an attempt to keep down the overall weight of the C.F. Just five coats of unpigmented dope, a bare minimum, were therefore applied by Rich and Karl.

Karl Heinzel assists Bill Stevenson as he makes some final adjustments. Interestingly, the cowling of the C.F. was screwed directly onto the underlying structure.

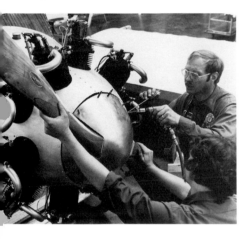

New parts incorporated into restored aircraft are marked as such, in order not to lead future historians and researchers astray.

Following the original practice, Karl Heinzel applied fabric to the wing tip at the point where the final wing covering will be attached. Here he brushes on a coat of varnish.

A modern aircraft dope was used rather than an early variety in the interest of safety, since the dopes of the Bellanca's day were highly flammable. Another departure from original methods was the use of modern wood glues which are permanent and, since they are not organic, are not subject to attack by fungus or insects, as are casein glues.

Among the visitors who had a close look at the monoplane were August T. Bellanca, his wife, Elettra, and their children Giselle, G. M., and Augie. It was with more than a little pleasure and pride that the restoration team showed them the airplane in much the same condition that Dorothy and Giuseppe Bellanca must have known it so many years ago. As this cabin monoplane was the only one on which the famous designer personally worked, it would no doubt have pleased him to know that his grandchildren would one day have the opportunity to sit in it.

In the course of the restoration, Rich and Karl became well aware that different parties had had a hand in the C.F. There was clear evidence of fast repairs and hastily performed modifications. Some of these changes showed both a lack of experience and judgment, as was the case with the absent firewall between the fuel tank and the engine. Giuseppe Bellanca would never have designed such an unsafe installation, and it may be assumed that there was indeed a firewall when the C.F. first took to the air. In sharp contrast to these modifications were the original parts of the plane, whose workmanship Rich Horigan pronounced "very, very good, the best of its time."

The magic of making an old airplane new is scarcely diminished by the time required for such an undertaking. Sixteen months and 3,911 man-hours of labor had been spent in the effort when the restored Bellanca C.F. was rolled out into the sunshine on May 13, 1980, and the pleasure experienced by museum craftsmen rivaled that which must have been felt by Giuseppe M. Bellanca himself sixty years earlier. Although well aware of its historic value, no one concerned with the project had realized what a lovely craft the C.F. would be.

Karl Heinzel and Rich Horigan apply fabric to the wing panels of the Bellanca C.F. The unusual concave form of the Bellanca wing may be seen in the nearer panel, which is upside down.

88

Rich Horigan shows August T. Bellanca the aircraft built by his father almost sixty years earlier.

Built in a time when registration numbers were not required, the Bellanca C.F. has only its name on the rudder.

With its round nose, exposed cylinders with curved exhaust stacks, and distinctive Bellanca propeller, the C.F. once more looks like the plane that competed with such success at air meets in 1922.

Photographed in front of one of the buildings at the Smithsonian's Paul E. Garber Facility, the Bellanca monoplane again looks fully flightworthy.

"The thing that surpised us most about the airplane," Karl Heinzel stated, "was that it came out looking so beautiful. When we got it we thought it would be ugly because it resembled a stagecoach with wings."

It sat resplendent in the spring sunshine, the absence of any but natural colors lending a look of gentle elegance. The hand-buffed wood glowed richly and sunlight reflected dazzlingly from the clear-doped fabric, or soaked through to reveal wing ribs like the veins in a leaf. Without a doubt, the C.F. is one of the prettiest aircraft of its period, its graceful lines far more appealing than the better-known Bellanca cabin monoplanes that followed it. Museum curators are frequently asked if restored aircraft are capable of flight. In the case of the Bellanca C.F., the answer is that little work would be required to bring it from display to flight status. Missing linkages and a throttle would have to be added, the engine would have to be flushed of preservatives and fuel and oil added, and cracks in the wing spars would need to be reinforced. In all probability, however, the plane will never fly again, as its historic value is too great.

The Bellanca C.F. is now displayed as a plane that brought about a significant change in the development of aviation in the United States, the patriarch of a line that helped to extend the bounds of commercial air travel around the world. It set heretofore unprecedented standards of efficiency and captured the imagination of millions of dreamers. The single greatest challenge remaining for this remarkable machine may well be to overcome the obscurity which has for so many years been its fate.

Notes

1. See *Blériot XI: The Story of a Classic Aircraft*, volume five in the Famous Aircraft of the National Air and Space Museum series (Washington, D.C.: Smithsonian Institution Press, 1982).

2. Clarence D. Chamberlin, *Record Flights* (Philadelphia: Dorrence and Company, 1928), pp. 279–80.

3. Ibid., pp. 208–9.

4. Ibid., p. 211.

5. Agreement between North Platte Aircraft Company and G. M. Bellanca, Bronx County, N.Y., April 29, 1921.

6. Statement by Harry G. Smith, Air Mail Service Pilot, Omaha, Neb., Nov. 27, 1922. See Appendix A for complete text.

7. Statement by William C. Hopson, Air Mail Service pilot, Omaha, Neb., Dec. 1, 1922. See Appendix A for complete text.

8. *Jane's All the World's Aircraft*, ed. C. G. Grey (London: Sampson, Low, Marston & Co., Ltd., 1923), p. 194b.

9. Statement by Harry G. Smith (note 6).

10. The ten cylinders of the Anzani engine were arranged in two banks of five, each on a separate ignition system. By turning off either magneto, the pilot could fly with just five of the ten cylinders producing power. The drag of the remaining cylinders reduced the engine output to less than half the normal horsepower.

11. Statement by William C. Hopson (note 7).

12. There are always exceptions to any generalization. For example, the Curtiss/ AEA Red Wing of 1908 had an enclosed pilot's seat.

13. Frank D. Hackett, First Lieutenant, U.S. Air Service, "Accident to Jacuzzi Monoplane," Engineering Division, Air Service, War Department, McCook Field, Ohio, July 18, 1921.

14. Ibid.

15. John Carisi to Robert S. Ament, Oct. 29, 1924.

16. William M. Leary, Jr., "Giuseppe Bellanca and the Search for 'Pure Streamline,'" *Aerospace Historian*, vol. 27, no. 3 (Fall/Sept. 1980), p. 190.

17. G. M. Bellanca to Colonel Paul Henderson, Second Assistant Postmaster General, Sept. 7, 1924.

18. G. M. Bellanca to Colonel Paul Henderson, Nov. 19, 1923.

19. Chamberlin, *Record Flights* (note 2), p. 15.

20. Ibid., p. 28.

21. Lauren D. Lyman, "Lindbergh's Flight: A Takeoff for Aviation," *Aerospace*, vol. 5, no. 5 (May 1967), p. 4.

22. Ibid., pp. 4–5.

23. G. M. Bellanca, foreword to Bellanca Company advertisement, Nov. 1, 1928.

24. Paul Kotze, interview with author, Dec. 3, 1980.

25. Paul E. Garber to Dorothy M. Bellanca, July 14, 1961.

26. Karl Heinzel, interview with author, Apr. 16, 1981.

Air Mail Field,
Omaha, Nebraska.
November 27, 1922

TO WHOM IT MAY CONCERN:

It was my privilege to give the Bellanca its first "hop."

The C. F. is a cabin type airplane capable of carrying four passengers and pilot with fuel for five hours' flight at ninety-five miles per hour.

The ease with which the plane is handled is extraordinary. The first time the plane was flown it was in perfect balance. I flew it then for its first twenty hours, and during that time no alignment was necessary. The plane has a rare combination of stability and maneuverability. On several occasions I flew it six or eight complete circles in a bank of about 30 degrees with hands off the stick controlling the plane entirely with the rudder. With the throttle at a cruising position the plane will fly hands-off without gaining or losing altitude. Open the throttle a little and the plane will slightly nose up and begin to climb. Close the throttle entirely and the plane will take a good normal gliding position. Together with this stability is a remarkable maneuverability. This plane will out maneuver planes of even much more horsepower. With the greatest ease it will loop, roll and wing-over. It goes into a spin with some difficulty and comes out extremely easy.

It is quite sensitive on the controls and yet not over sensitive. It can be side-slipped very close to the ground and easily taken out of the slip and landed. This makes it a very good plane to get into small fields. In fact it is the most correctly balanced and easiest handled plane I ever flew.

The first flight that was made with a load I made with 625 pounds of sand in the cabin. The plane took this load off very easily and I am convinced that it will carry in addition to the weight of the pilot and full fuel capacity, 700 or 750 pounds of pay load. With a full load the speed of the plane seems to be practically the same as when empty and the plane handles with the same ease and the balance is just as good.

The cabin was made for comfort. It is as large and roomy as an ordinary four passenger enclosed automobile. There is ample room for four passengers to be seated comfortably and with plenty of leg room. The door is large enough for easy entrance and exit.

One of the best features of the Bellanca is its combination of high cruising speed, quick take-off, low landing speed, and large gliding ratio. As has been stated the cruising speed is 95 m.p.h. and the landing speed is 30 m.p.h. The gliding ratio is about 12 to 1 and the take-off is very short. This combination makes the plane ideal for cross-country and commercial flying.

I believe the Bellanca is the most efficient plane built. The plane will carry 650 pounds or more of pay load at a cruising speed of 95 m.p.h. on a gasoline consumption of 6 gallons per hour. This economy of operation together with its combination of low landing speed, large gliding ratio, large comfortable cabin with ease of exit and entrance, and ease of handling, makes the Bellanca the safest and most efficient plane built today.

Yours truly,

Harry G. Smith
Pilot, Air Mail Service,
Omaha, Nebraska

94

Air Mail Field,
Omaha, Nebraska
December 1, 1922

TO WHOM IT MAY CONCERN:

On being asked to fly the Bellanca C. F. monoplane last July I accepted very readily, mainly to satisfy my curiosity, having heard a great deal about the remarkable performance of this new plane.

During my flying experience of six years, in that time traveling about 225,000 miles or 2600 hours actual flying time in air, and flying about 25 different makes of planes, I had heard a great many of these remarkable claims for new planes, to find out that they had been greatly exaggerated. Therefore when I went out to take my initial hop in the Bellanca I was in a skeptical mood with eyes open for defects and faults rather than good qualities.

My first ride lasted 45 minutes during which time I put her through her paces. I went up a skeptic but came down a firm believer in the Bellanca C.F. She was by far the most remarkable performing plane I had ever flown or dreamed of flying. Since that time I have flown her about 40 hours and each flight has strengthened my belief in this plane. For climb, speed, gliding, weight carrying and ease of operation under all conditions of practical flying she is years ahead of any plane in the world today.

Although the owners of this plane have been very conservative about weight carrying, the actual pay load carried being 650 lbs., beside pilot, I firmly believe that this plane will successfully fly with a pay load of 1000 lbs. With a pay load of 550 lbs. I have maintained a horizontal flight with five cylinders shut off, using only about 35 H.P. Although this plane is very light it is exceptionally strong and will handle very nicely both in air and landing and take-off in very heavy adverse wind conditions. She can be taken off and landed in very small fields and with her remarkable climbing ability will get over high obstructions at edge of field.

The Anzani motor used I have found to be a very reliable and rugged power plant, and is so well installed that the ship is remarkably free from vibration. The cabin of the Bellanca is roomy and comfortably seats four passengers and the noise has been reduced so that it is possible for the pilot to talk to the passengers who are at least four feet ahead.

I flew this plane in two air meets, one at Tarkio, Mo., July 25–28, 1922 and at Norfolk, Nebraska, August 27–29th, where we entered contests competing with the best planes in the country with motors of more than double and triple the motor used in the Bellanca. I won seven first prizes in these two meets, each contest being virtually a walk-away for the Bellanca. At Norfolk the official time for the Bellanca in a speed contest over a three point course, three laps of 10 miles each, was 109 m.p.h. This speed was made with a Jenny prop of only five ft. pitch, having broken our regular propeller of 7 ft. 11 in. pitch with which I made unofficial speed of 115 m.p.h.

In a climbing contest at Tarkio, I arrived at 2000 feet altitude in 2 min. when a Fokker who was the nearest competitor was at 1700 feet. In a gliding contest I remained in the air for 5 min. 20 sec. after shutting off all power at 2000 feet altitude.

At Norfolk we entertained the crowd with two aerial weddings in the Bellanca. With the bride and groom, minister and best man, I left the ground after a run of 200 feet against practically no head wind.

Yours very truly,

William C. Hopson
Pilot, Air Mail Service,
Omaha, Nebraska

APPENDIX **B** Specifications and
Performance

	Bellanca C.F., 1922		Bellanca CH Pacemaker, 1932	
Wing span:	40 ft 0 in	12.20 m	47 ft 6 in	14.48 m
Length:	23 ft 10 in	7.26 m	27 ft 11 in	8.53 m
Height:	7 ft 3 in	2.21 m	8 ft 4 in	2.54 m
Empty weight:	950 lbs	432 kgs	2,420 lbs	1,098 kgs
Gross weight:	1,990 lbs	908 kgs	4,300 lbs	1,954 kgs
Useful load:	1,040 lbs	475 kgs	1,880 lbs	853 kgs
Wing area:	290 ft²	27 m²	285 ft²	26.47 m²
Wing loading:	6.86 lbs/ft²	3.11 kgs/ft²	15.1 lbs/ft²	6.85 kgs/ft²
Power loading:	22 lbs/hp	10 kgs/hp	14.3 lbs/hp	6.49 kgs/hp
Stall speed:	40 mph	65 km/h	53 mph	85 km/h
Cruise speed:	95 mph	152 km/h	125 mph	200 km/h
Maximum speed:	110 mph	176 km/h	150 mph	240 km/h
Initial rate of climb:	600 ft/min	185 m/min	900 ft/min	275 m/min
Service ceiling:	16,000 ft	4,875 m	17,000 ft	5,180 m
Range:	480 mi	770 km	850 mi	1,360 km
Fuel capacity:	35 U.S. gal.	133.1	120 U.S. gal	456 1.
Engine:	Anzani 10-cylinder air-cooled radial engine, 90 hp.		Wright J6 Whirlwind 9-cylinder air-cooled radial engine, 300 hp.	

ABOUT THE AUTHOR:

JAY P. SPENSER is the author of three books and a number of articles in major aviation magazines. A graduate of Middlebury College, he has had a lifelong love of flight. He has been a researcher and writer in the Aeronautics Department of the National Air and Space Museum since 1976, and is the author of *Aeronca C-2: The Story of the Flying Bathtub*, an earlier volume in this series.